99 WAYS
TO TEACH
LIKE THE
MASTER

99 WAYS
TO TEACH
LIKE THE
MASTER

BY

T.J. BURDICK

EN ROUTE BOOKS & MEDIA

En Route Books & Media

Print ISBN: 978-1-950108-58-9
E-book ISBN: 978-1-63337-027-2

Contact us at contactus@enroutebooksandmedia.com

This book is dedicated to Jesus, my beloved Teacher.
To my wife, Maribel, my best friend.

En Route would like to give a special note of thanks to T.J. Burdick for his cover design and to Michael Stevens for his logo design.

"Hold fast to instruction, never let her go; keep her, for she is your life."
–Proverbs 4:13

CONTENTS

FOREWORD
PATRICK S.J. CARMACK, J.D.

In this book, author T.J. Burdick reminds us of our need to base education on something other than our wits, our personal insights or clever techniques. Each of 99 short readings begins with Sacred Scripture and accompanying meditations for teachers, set forth in familiar, contemporary language easily accessible to educators – parents and teachers – on all levels.

With a sure hand borne from practical teaching experience, the author explores many lessons and examples from which educators can profit. The readings, anecdotes and examples are carefully selected by the author to be specifically relevant to educators of all stripes, and remind us that teaching is first a labor of love, and so is best learned from the words and example of our Divine Teacher, Jesus Christ, the King of Love.

Over and again in the history of education, the discovery of some new – and often helpful – pedagogical technique or insight has so captured the imaginations of educators with its possibilities that they have lost sight of the essentials. If it is not going to become arid and sterile, we need to base Christian education on its Biblical and patristic moorings.

What many scholars believe was the height of education and pedagogy – the Aristotelian-Thomistic synthesis taught in the scholastic, dialectical method of the High Middle Ages – began its decline by abandoning Biblical commentary in favor of disputing subtle questions with novel approaches neither rooted in Sacred Scripture nor the Fathers of the Church. Unlike all of the Fathers and St. Thomas Aquinas (d.1274), neither of the great scholastics John Duns Scotus (d.1308) nor William of Ockham (d.1347) wrote Biblical commentaries – there, around A.D. 1300, began the decline from the heights.

After having been somewhat neglected by scholars during the next two centuries of intellectual decline in the West, Gutenberg and other printers made the Bible widely available by the end of the 15th century. The Bible was not then "rediscovered" – that was a calumny against the Church – it had never been lost and throughout that period was always in daily liturgical use throughout the universal Church. But the invention of movable type did make it far more widely available. In a brief space of time, innumerable editions, especially of the Latin Vulgate, poured from the press and were diffused throughout the Catholic world. Pope Clement V established chairs of Oriental literature in the principal universities of Europe helping Catholics to make more accurate translations from the original texts of the Bible, as well as of the Latin version.

However, with the decline of scholasticism the newly published Bible was also handed over to some theologians and laity who were influenced by the errors (such as nominalism) spreading in the wake of the collapse of the medieval intellectual synthesis mentioned above. The countless, often conflicting, interpretations of critical Biblical passages, stemming mainly from the Reformers, attest to that fact, as does their departure from traditional, patristic understandings of many difficult passages, resulting in the birth of numerous Protestant churches. Partly in reaction to errors, and partly in its role as the repository of Sacred Scripture, the Church, especially after the Council of Trent, gradually initiated

3

numerous endeavors to spread a correct understanding of the Bible.

More recently, but as part of the same Catholic response, the *École Biblique* was founded in 1890 in Jerusalem and has been involved in the exegesis of biblical texts. It has carried out related archaeological research and in the principle disciplines of Biblical studies. The scholars at the school have been heavily involved in the translation and interpretation of the Dead Sea scrolls. In 1893 Pope Leo XIII issued the encyclical *Providentissimus Deus* on the study of Holy Scripture and pointed out the errors of the rationalists and "higher critics," and explained how apparent contradictions between science and religion could be reconciled. In 1902, Pope Leo also instituted the Pontifical Biblical Commission to modernize Catholic Biblical studies. A few years later St. Pius X commended the society of St. Jerome, which strives to promote among the faithful the custom of reading and meditating on the Gospels. In 1907, Pope Pius XI founded in Rome the Benedictine monastery of St. Jerome, devoted exclusively to Biblical studies. Pope Benedict XV exhorted "all the children of the Church…to reverence the Holy Scripture, to read it piously and meditate it constantly," so "that there is no Christian family any more without them and that all are accustomed to read and meditate them daily." Every Pope since has promoted the study of the Bible, as did the Dogmatic Constitution Dei Verbum (The Word of God), promulgated by Vatican Council II in 1963.

Why this heavy emphasis by the Church on Biblical studies? Because as St. Jerome said long ago: "Ignorance of Scripture is ignorance of Christ," and, as Pope Benedict XVI said to the leaders of Catholic higher education in the United States in 2008, "fostering personal intimacy with Jesus Christ and communal witness to his loving truth is indispensable to Catholic institutions of learning."

Could any stronger formal ecclesiastical exhortations than

the foregoing, some directed specifically to Catholic educators, to read, study and meditate on the Bible be imagined? And do not these exhortations also point to the ancient order to prayer, the *lectio divina* ("sacred reading"), beginning with reading Scripture, then thinking/meditating on the reading, leading to prayer? As Simon Tugwell, O.P. has noted elsewhere, that ancient order to prayer is found in Hugh of St. Victor, St. Thomas Aquinas, *The Nine Ways of Prayer* of St. Dominic, in Guigo the Carthusian and in *The Cloud of Unknowing*.

Yet the Catechism states that "the Christian faith is not a 'religion of the book.' Christianity is the religion of the 'Word' of God, a word which is 'not a written and mute word, but the Word is incarnate and living.' If the Scriptures are not to remain a dead letter, Christ, the eternal Word of the living God, must, through the Holy Spirit, 'open minds' to understand the Scriptures." That is why to the traditional practices mentioned above – reading, thinking, praying – was often added (or understood as the culmination thereof) "contemplation," prayer in which the soul is lifted up by and in the Holy Spirit to experience that personal intimacy with Jesus Christ and God the Father.

As Pope Benedict XVI also said to the leaders of Catholic education, mentioned above: "God's desire to make himself known, and the intimate desire of all human beings to know the truth, provide the context for human inquiry into the meaning of life. This unique encounter is sustained within our Christian community: the one who seeks the truth becomes the one who lives by faith. It can be described as a move from 'I' to 'we,' leading the individual to be numbered among God's people."

As Papal biographer George Weigel has written, "Catholic higher education in the twenty-first century can also help the Western world retain its cultural memory, which is in danger of being lost under the pressures of 'relevance' and an overwrought worry about developing marketable skills." This can best be done by a "heavy (and required) emphasis on an encounter with the classics, including that classic of biblical religion, the Bible."

This book then, is right in line with the ancient Christian tradition of *lectio divina* and with numerous Papal exhortations – including those specifically directed to Catholic educators – to read and meditate on Sacred Scripture – the greatest of the Great Books. It is specifically designed for teachers by the author to help them do that, with meditations based on the example of Christ the Divine Teacher.

Patrick S.J. Carmack, J.D.

Founder and President,
The Angelicum Academy (angelicum.net)
The Great Books Academy (greatbooksacademy.org)

St. John of the Cross, A.D. 2014

How To Read This Book

Teachers have a lot on their plates. Think of this book as that plate. It was created to form in the reader a solid foundation through which all of your teaching can be transformed by Christ.

To create this meal, each section has a specific recipe to follow:

Scripture- Jesus is known as the *Living Bread* and *the Word made Flesh*. His life as transmitted through the Gospels represents the main course for our spiritual diet.

Reflection- I've prepared a short, one-minute long reflection that will take Christ's life and make it part of yours. Like silverware, they take the Gospels to your tongue so that your soul can digest every morsel.

Eat well!

INTRODUCTION

In my decades of teaching experience, I have been introduced to a myriad of delivery strategies, management techniques, intervention ideologies and even public speaking tips. While some of these have proven to be very effective, there are very few I would consider to have been fruitful.

Even in education, there is money to be made by the "newest thing" and the latest "research-based" fad. Sadly, much of my time has been squandered at empty professional development seminars listening to people try to sell me something as opposed to making me a better teacher.

It wasn't until I began reading the Gospels that I realized that all of the educational training I found to be effective was already practiced by Jesus over 2,000 years ago.

Think about it: who was the top chemist at the Wedding in Cana? Jesus: He changed the molecular structure of water into wine!

Who was the best mathematician in all of Judea? Jesus: He could multiply bread and fish!

Who gave the finest incentive if you listened to his teachings? Jesus: He promised us eternal life.

For centuries the world of education has done its best to invent the newest and most effective means of teaching students, but we sometimes get so caught up in these trends that we fail to recognize what the author of the Old Testament book of Ecclesiastes knew, that simply "there is nothing new under the sun."[1] Indeed from the very beginning, it was Jesus Christ who taught us all how to teach effectively.

---

1 *The Holy Bible: Revised Standard Version Catholic Edition*, Eccles. 1:9

THE ESSENTIALS

According to the research of psychologist Abraham Maslow, all people, young and old, need to sustain a hierarchy of certain needs.

The most important levels of our needs are made up of the most basic needs... Needs at the bottom of this "pyramid" are basic physical requirements including the need for food, water, sleep and warmth. Once these lower-level needs have been met, people can move on to the next level of needs, which include safety, to love/belong, to esteem and finally to self actualization.[2]

In less psychologically-sounding verbiage, make sure you and your kids are surviving. Without the basics of food, shelter and sleep, there is no way they will be able to find "x" in your algebra lesson. If you feel like jumping into your car without your keys, go ahead! But you won't get very far!

If you don't have the essentials of life, you really don't have life at all.

Strangely enough, basic survival is the foundation of the Gospel message. How often did Christ feed the hungry, eat with the lowly and cure the sick? It was almost as if His entire ministry

2 Kendra Cherry, "Hierarchy of Needs: The Five Levels of Maslow's Hierarchy of Needs" *About.com Guide*. (4 Jan 2015), at http://psychology.about.com

involved getting the downtrodden to a point that they could sustain themselves and then, follow Him.

We have to ask ourselves: *What do I need to be an effective teacher? What are the basic needs I need to survive?*

1. Prayer

In the beginning was the Word, and the Word was with God, and the Word was God.
- John 1:1

Pope Francis tells us that "Faith is our response to a word which engages us personally, to a 'Thou' who calls us by name."[3] This "Thou" is Jesus, or as St. John refers to Him: the Word made flesh.

The primary mode for Christian communication is prayer. Prayer takes on various forms: the liturgy, the rosary, contemplative and meditative, penitential etc. What we sometimes forget is that our human minds are incapable of praying correctly (Romans 8:26). In all humility, it is not we who begin the dialogue we know as prayer; rather, it was God who began communicating with us even before we were born. Our response to this call is true prayer. Everything else is a construct of our imagination.

†††

I recall when I was a teenager and my prayers consisted of my talking for five minutes about the things I wanted. Then, I would conjure up a voice in my head that I told myself was God: He would agree with all of my requests and I would return to

---

3 Pope Francis, Encyclical Letter of the Supreme Pontiff to the Bishops Priests and Deacons Consecrated Persons and the Lay Faithful on Faith, *Lumen Fidei,* §8

my daily schedule waiting for my desires to be met. When they weren't, I had to re-think my strategy.

It wasn't until I began praying in silence that I understood what quality prayer was. That's when I found that my mind was not the starting point for celestial conversation, it was only a small stop in the eternal wavelength that began with God and rippled through His entire creation.

The most essential aspect of your mission as teacher is to know, love and pursue Truth through Jesus. He is the Master of the universe, the Creative genius that was behind the making of you, everyone you love and everything in this world.

Ensure that you respond to His constant call to educate your children properly through consistent, daily prayer.

2. Family

The book of the genealogy of Jesus Christ, the son of David, the son of Abraham. Abraham was the father of Isaac...
So all the generations from Abraham to David were fourteen generations, and from David to the depor-tation to Babylon fourteen generations, and from the deportation to Babylon to the Christ fourteen gener-ations.
- Matt. 1:1, 17

In the beginning part of the first lesson of Matthew is a ge-nealogy. The names listed there refer to the past men that make up the family tree of Jesus. This family history begins with some familiar Old Testament names such as Abraham, Isaac, Jacob and Judah. Towards the middle, David and Solomon come into the picture amongst a slew of unfamiliar names. Finally, Jesus completes the genealogical study with Mary and Joseph mentioned as His mother and father.

In hind sight, some of Jesus' relatives were accomplished leaders while others were, well, forgetful. Regardless of their deeds, each person played a central part in the development of God's plan for His people. If one of these people were missing from the list of Jesus' family tree, the history of salvation would not have been the same.

†††

In a similar way, if one of our students was missing from our learning environment, it wouldn't be the same. Regardless of the impression they might give us, God has brought them to us for a reason that might not be realized until well into the future. That reason is their salvation. Each student thus becomes a part of us as teachers and, to the same extent that God considers you His son or daughter, so you should consider your students part of that same family.

Your group is a sprouting branch that needs protection, nourishment and light. May our lessons pay homage to the root of our spiritual family tree – Jesus – and may He bless our students and us with a great quantity of fruit throughout the year.

3. Fiat

And he came to her and said, "Hail, full of grace, the Lord is with you!" And behold, you will conceive in your womb and bear a son, and you shall call his name Jesus. And Mary said, "Behold, I am the handmaid of the Lord; let it be to me according to your word." And the angel departed from her.
- Luke 1:28, 31, 38

We all have strengths. We tend to find ways to capitalize on these strengths and ensure success in whatever we do. Since we were given these strengths by God for a reason, it seems logical that we would use them to achieve more for His Kingdom. For example, I'm a talented linguist. I speak English and Spanish fluently and I am very effective at teaching in two languages.

However, there are times when we will be required to step outside of our comfortable boxes where our strengths are. When this happens, we will confront what is unordinary and perhaps difficult to us. As a result, we will have some of our weaknesses exposed. In my case, I have been asked to teach several science classes during my career. I got Cs in science, if I was lucky, throughout high school and college. It is difficult for me, to say the least.

Mary became the vessel for the most precious gift God has ever given to the world – His Son, Jesus Christ. Mary was surely embracing the uncomfortable pregnant lifestyle as she carried the Son of God within her womb. However, to make the situation unordinary, she was given this role not through the means of regular human intercourse. Rather, she was blessed with this extraordinary gift by means of the Holy Spirit.

✝✝✝

Mary's role is a constant reminder for us humans to accept God's gifts even when we find them unorthodox. Without her, Jesus would never have been able to step outside of heaven and share His love with all of humanity.

Your students are unique. They will require you to teach in different ways, ask different questions, and inspire through different means than others. As we create new lesson plans and brainstorm different activities, it is important to remember that, although our weaknesses might be exposed at times, our mission remains the same – we are to say "fiat," or "yes," to Christ's call to instruct our children well, even if that means we have to teach them science.

4. Clothes

And while they were there, the time came for her to be delivered. And she gave birth to her first-born son and wrapped him in swaddling cloths, and laid him in a manger, because there was no place for them in the inn.
- Luke 2:6-7

We believe that God is the ultimate and infinite good. In an act that goes beyond our understanding, God sent His only Son, Jesus, down to earth. Humbly clothed in the uncomfortable chill of human flesh, He was welcomed into the world by being wrapped in the warmth of His mother's swaddling clothes.

Biblically, Jesus' garbs always seem to have special spiritual significance. At His birth, the swaddling clothes were a King's robe that He will eventually grow into. The woman with hemorrhages was healed by touching His clothes,[4] and the soldiers casted lots for His bloodied garments while He was being crucified.[5] With such a demand for his attire, you'd think He would have ended up on a catwalk instead of Calvary!

†††

We too have power in the way we dress. At first glance, our students and colleagues make judgments about who we are by the clothes we wear. For most people, the way we dress is a reflection

---

4 Mark 5:25-34
5 Matt. 27:35

of our personality and our identity.

However, as educators we also have a separate, more sub-liminal reason for dressing the way we do. Although we dress according to our personalities, we also dress in a way that we would want our students to dress in the future. As our students learn to be successful and responsible, we model a dress code that they might use to distinguish themselves as successful and flourishing scholars.

Regardless of whether or not we wear a tie or a dress, slacks or skirts, loafers, high heels, or sneakers (for all the gym teachers out there) to school every day, we must dress ourselves first in humility and modesty, then in our material clothes. For we "clothe ourselves as one as holy and beloved by God."[6]

Just as Jesus' clothes had the significant power, so too do our clothes.

5. Food

[Mary and Joseph] laid him in a manger, because there was no place for them in the inn.
- Luke 2:7

Food has a universal way of educating us. It teaches us to want, to wait, and to satisfy our physical cravings on a daily basis. It captures all five senses and, it gives us life through the invisible effects that it has on our body during digestion.

Invisible effects... wait a minute! Our faith has millions of invisible effects. No wonder Jesus used food in almost all of His greatest lessons; He wanted to teach us how to be faithful!

After being swaddled in Mary's garments, Christ was laid in His first resting place, a feeding trough for animals, also known as

---

6 Col. 3:12

a manger. It was there, in a place where wild animals ate, that He would foretell the name He gave to Himself, the Bread of Life,[7] and become food for all who hunger for righteousness.

†††

The physical need for sustenance is a phenomenal catalyst for learning. In fact, the best resources you need to get your point across can be found in your refrigerator. I've found that fruits make great planets for solar system models and I'm pretty sure pizza is the only way a growing boy will ever appreciate fractions.

Satisfying their physical needs can easily allow you to link learning with the senses which, in the long run, can create longer memory retention.[8] If the food is nutritious, you score a double whammy for making their bodies last longer too!

On the spiritual level, however, we must maintain an even healthier lifestyle than we do physically. We have to watch what we "eat," so to speak, when it comes to our soul's survival. We must be aware of the fast food distractions that make us fat with misinformation and lazy through malnutrition. If we really want our souls to thrive, we must allow God to feed us through silent prayer, study and service.

Now then, the question that you must ask yourself is: *what are you feeding your student(s)*? Are you serving them the appetizer of academics, the side dish of a good example, and the main course of Christ's gospel message? Or are you starving them into spiritual malnutrition?

You be the judge. Better yet, you be the chef!

---

7 John 6:35

8 Egg Nutrition Center, The, *Choline: The "New" Essential Nutrient, Nutrition Close-Up Special Report*, (4 Jan 2015), at <http://www.cholineinfo.org>

6. Gifts

Now when Jesus was born in Bethlehem of Judea in the days of Herod the king, behold, wise men from the East came to Jerusalem, saying, "Where is he who has been born king of the Jews? For we have seen his star in the East, and have come to worship him."
When they saw the star, they rejoiced exceedingly with great joy; and going into the house they saw the child with Mary his mother, and they fell down and worshipped him. Then, opening their treasures, they offered him gifts, gold and frankincense and myrrh. And being warned in a dream not to return to Herod, they departed to their own country by another way.
- Matt. 2:1-2, 10-12

Since the beginning of time, people have looked to the night skies to see the stars. We have used them to explain our traditions, predict our futures, and like the Magi, guide us through the darkness of the night.

The Magi have commonly been referred to as "The Three Wise Men." This term comes from the common interpretation that they were astrologers and dream interpreters in their distant land of Persia.[9] So well did they watch the skies that they were ordered by King Herod to share their information with him and then search for the prophesized "ruler" in Bethlehem. Little did these highly educated men know how "overjoyed" they would be at following this particular star through the darkness.

When they arrived, they came bearing gifts because their intellects understood the significance of Christ's birth. Gold, frankincense and myrrh became synonymous with our personal talents

---

9 Walter Drum, "Magi." The Catholic Encyclopedia. Vol. 9. (New York: Robert Appleton Company, 1910), 27. Jan. 2015 <http://www.newadvent.org/cathen/09527a.htm>

that we offer God in return for giving us life, intelligence, and free will. Like the Magi, we give back to the Creator what is rightfully His. In return, we are overjoyed at seeing His face!

†††

Finding Christ requires a life-long spiritual journey. This pilgrimage is manifested in what Vygostsy calls the Zone of Proximal Development.[10] This term refers to the fact that if a student is instructed below or above what they are able to handle academically, red flags go up in their brains and learning cannot occur.

You wouldn't teach an English Literature Major from Harvard the proper pronunciation of basic colors. Nor would you instruct a three year old how to write iambic pentameter. These tasks would be outside of their ZPDs.

The same holds true for spiritual knowledge. As our students search for ways to understand truth, their best tool is the same as the Magi – their education. The intelligence they gain throughout their education will allow them to move across their spiritual ZPD and thus recognize the Master's gifts in their lives. Ultimately they will become overjoyed wise men and women when they finally see Christ at the end of their journey, just like the Three Kings.

All they need is a star to guide them.

7. Obedience

Now when they had departed, behold, an angel of the Lord appeared to Joseph in a dream and said, "Rise, take the child and his mother, and flee to Egypt, and remain there till I tell you; for Herod is about to search

---

10 Lev Vygotsky, *Interaction between learning and development. Mind and society* (Cambridge: Harvard University Press, 1978)

for the child, to destroy him." And he rose and took the child and his mother by night, and departed to Egypt, and remained there until the death of Herod. This was to fulfill what the Lord had spoken by the prophet, "Out of Egypt have I called my son."
- Matt. 2:13-15

After almost divorcing his wife, then trekking across the desert with his pregnant love, only to have the baby born in the worst of conditions, he was told to flee with his postpartum wife and newborn into the desert of Egypt. There, he was to fulfill his obligation as a husband to a mysterious woman and raise a child that was not genetically his. Furthermore, he had the job of explaining the world to the "man/God" who invented it and to live alongside the only other person besides his adopted Son who was born without original sin. Poor Joseph.

Although Joseph's role in Sacred Scripture is fairly silent (he is only briefly mentioned in the Gospels of Matthew and Luke), it is pivotal that we take the spirit of his actions into our own daily lives. This spirit is one of obedience to our God. Had it not been for Joseph's ability to overcome his own pride and accept the will of God, the very life of Jesus would have been put in danger. Such an obedient spirit manifests itself inside our learning environments every single day we teach.

†††

We exercise a degree of power over our students. This power is a gift from God and, in order for it to be useful, our students must learn to be obedient. In return, our vow of obedience to God will give us the grace necessary to make the best decisions possible so that the obedient student can learn from the obedient teacher.

When a group establishes such trust, a sacred unity is established that is similar to that of the Holy Family. Like Joseph, we might not understand why we are placed in some positions, but in the spirit of faith and obedience, we will lead our students towards truth. Like Egypt was for the Holy Family, so shall our learning environments be places of refuge and constant reflection on the spiritual truths that we both learn and teach.

"Unless he obeys, a man cannot believe." ~Dietrich Bonhoeffer

8. Zeal

When they did not find him, they returned to Jerusalem, seeking him. After three days they found him in the temple, sitting among the teachers, listening to them and asking them questions; and all who heard him were amazed at his understanding and his answers. And when they saw him they were astonished; and his mother said to him, "Son, why have you treated us so? Behold, your father and I have been looking for you anxiously." And he said to them, "How is it that you sought me? Did you not know that I must be in my Father's house?" And they did not understand the saying which he spoke to them. And he went down with them and came to Nazareth, and was obedient to them; and his mother kept all these things in her heart. And Jesus increased in wisdom and in stature, and in favor with God and man.
- Luke 2:45-52

I once took a class called Mexican Culture and Geography. I hated Spanish at the time but at the end of the semester, those who passed would go to Mexico. So, I agreed to take the class for the sole reason that I would score a nice Christmas vacation trip.

I passed. I went. And I met some of the most impressive bilingual servants I have ever come in contact with. While at first they were only the crutch I needed for translation purposes, they quickly became the catalysts for a great change in my heart. Their passion for people spread across the obstacles of language and culture that before that point, I refused to overcome.

Three weeks after the trip, I switched my major to Spanish and my world has never been the same.

†††

The energy and interest that we dedicate to our lessons will set the tone for our students to catch the contagious fire of interest that we emanate, much like the companions from my mission trip to Mexico and the Rabbis that Jesus listened to in the temple. The key to this process is our zeal.

St. John Baptist De La Salle tells us in his ninth meditation for the time of retreat:

"You must not doubt that it is a great gift of God, this grace he has given you to be entrusted with the instruction of children, to announce the Gospel to them and to bring them up in the spirit of religion. But in calling you to this holy ministry, God demands that you fulfill it with ardent zeal for their salvation, because this is the work of God, and he curses the one who does his work carelessly."[11]

Our students are filled with passion, questions and eagerness to become something special, just like Jesus was in His youth. It would do us well to command their interest with enthusiasm, passion, and zeal much like the teachers in the Temple.

---

11 St. John Baptist De La Salle, *Meditations for the Time of Retreat* (Rouen, France 1730), at http://www.lasallian.info

9. Water

In those days Jesus came from Nazareth of Galilee and was baptized by John in the Jordan. And when he came up out of the water, immediately he saw the heavens opened and the Spirit descending upon him like a dove; and a voice came from heaven, "Thou art my beloved Son; with thee I am well pleased."
- Mark 1:9-11

The term "food for thought" has been synonymous with learning since its inception. Logically, whatever makes us think gives us educational nutrition. If "food," then, can be compared to our academic flourishing, why not water?

When we are baptized, we are initiated into God's family. Through this ceremony, we defeat sin and acknowledge God as our spiritual Father. As a result, we are considered sons and daughters of God.

Jesus had absolutely no reason to be baptized under the context of repentance by which John the Baptist preached. What would the Son of God in His perfection need to repent from? Jesus was baptized for other reasons – one of which was to ready His soul for the mission that was ahead of Him. It was so important to His ministry that He be cleansed by the waters of the Jordan because it was then that the heavens were "torn open" and "the Spirit descended upon Him like a dove." His humanity and the Spirit of God became submitted to each other. His soul was now ready for His mission.

†††

While we carry out this mission, it would be in our best interest to remember that whatever "food for thought" that we provide for our students must be accompanied by the sacramental water of our baptism. It is through this sacrament that we unite our human weakness to God's omnipotence.

So what do you need to be an effective teacher? What are the basic needs you need to survive?

Prayer
Family
Fiat
Clothes
Food
Gifts
Obedience
Zeal
Water

At this moment, people are buying top-model curriculums, taking out loans to pay for their college preparatory program and buying zillions of resources to become better teachers. Some of what they buy/learn will be useful, but truthfully, the aforementioned list is all you really need to get started.

It's all Jesus needed.

Harold Copping, "Jesus at the Home of Mary and Martha," 1927
– Wikimedia Commons

His Educational Philosophy

Jesus spent the first 30 years of His earthly life in evangelical silence. As far as we know, He did not heal his friends' skinned knees, multiply His mother's homemade bread when visitors arrived, nor scratch down archetypes of prayer methods. It wasn't until He was well into adulthood that He began His ministry which leads us to believe that He spent the majority of His early life contemplating what He was going to do and why He was going to do it.

The "why" is the most important part of an educator's mission. It is the preemptive act that solidifies our motivation and coerces our passions into fitting the mold of God's will. Why we teach is precisely the same reason why Jesus taught: to attain salvation for the souls of His students.

The following Gospel excerpts reiterate the reasons why Christ became our teacher and how we can go about creating our own educational philosophies based on His timeless model.

10. Establishing Vision

And passing along by the Sea of Galilee, he saw Si-

*mon and Andrew the brother of Simon casting a net
in the sea; for they were fishermen. And Jesus said to
them, "Follow me and I will make you become fishers
of men." And immediately they left their nets and followed him.*
- Mark 1:16-18

Jesus' words tend to have an unorthodox effect on those
to whom He is speaking. Jesus tells His first disciples that they
would be "fishers of men" if they were to follow Him.

The truth is that it isn't what Jesus said that made them re-
act the way they did: it was *how* He said it. The voice of Jesus
rang into His first apostles, but the vibrations touched their souls
when He said, *"Come, I will make you fishers of men."* With such
confidence and calmness, Jesus offered to them a way of life that
involved not only mystery, but also vision. In the back of their
minds they knew that this loner on the shore knew what He was
talking about, and they needed to follow Him.

Our students will recognize very quickly if we, like Jesus,
have a vision for them. It is of great importance that we develop this vision, then speak and act with great confidence in our
abilities to teach them this vision. Like Jesus, we must radiate an
impression of peaceful confidence that touches the souls of our
students to the point that they will know that if they follow us,
they will be successful regardless of how mysterious or difficult
the path may be.

Take a few moments before teaching and decide what your
vision is for your students. What do we want them to accomplish?
What expectations will you set to make sure they become successful beyond your instruction? What individual goals do they have
for themselves?

When we implement our vision into the hearts of our students and unify our efforts with theirs, we too will be "fishers of

men," just like Jesus.

Don't be surprised if they think you are a little nuts though.

Before you begin establishing that vision, identify which of the following attributes of an effective teacher you consider to be your strengths and which you consider to be your weakness. Knowing your abilities will help you create a framework that works for both you and your kiddos.

THE ATTRIBUTES OF AN
EFFECTIVE TEACHER

11. Humility

Blessed are the poor in spirit, for theirs is the kingdom of heaven.
- Matt. 5:3

The skeleton for a truly effective educator is found at the heart of Christ's Sermon on the Mount, the Beatitudes. The word beatitude means "a wish or desire that all good fortune, especially of a spiritual or supernatural."[12] But to find the true meaning, we must go back to its original Latin, *beatitudinem*. This word is a conjunction of the two words beatus, which means "blessed or happy," and beare which means "to make happy." Therefore, it is not good enough to be happy, but we must also make happiness be.

Jesus instructs us indirectly on how to do this. He tells us that the kingdom of heaven belongs to those who are "poor in spirit."

In the Old Testament, poverty was not looked upon solely as

---

12 Patrick Morrisroe, "Blessing." The Catholic Encyclopedia. Vol. 2. New York: Robert Appleton Company, 1907. 27 Jan. 2015 <http://www.newadvent.org/cathen/02599b.htm>

being without material possessions. It was also seen as a humble lifestyle that led people closer to God. Although the poor suffered physically due to their economic detriment, they were able to draw closer to their faith for that same reason. After all, the less you rely on the world, the more you rely on God. With less possessions to distract them, they were thankful when they received His physical graces of food, shelter etc. As a result, they could recognize His face in every blessing they received.

†††

Many people have figured out that being educated can lead to financial success. This is correct, but the true foundation of the Gospel message goes against that current. It moves us to be "poor in spirit," to be humble from within, to grow closer to God in everything we do regardless of our economic status. This is because those with fewer possessions understand this better than most because they have less to distract them.

Remember, it was Lazarus who was comforted in the afterlife because he had nothing, while the rich man suffered though he had much.[13] Perhaps this is why Jesus came to us as a humble, carpenter's Son?

Perhaps this is why you are a teacher?

12. Fortitude

Blessed are those who mourn, for they shall be comforted.
- Matt. 5:4

During the last years of his life, St. Thomas Aquinas wrote

---

13 Luke 16:19-31

the following in his masterpiece, *The Shorter Summa*:

"God alone is His own goodness and He alone is essentially good. All other beings are said to be good according as they participate, to some extent, in Him."[14]

In other words, God and all of His creation (humans included) are, in essence, good.

On the other hand, we can't deny that pain exists in our world. Natural disasters, war, economic crisis, poverty and other evils have made their presence known quite clearly in today's world. Hence, the question resounds, "*If God is so good, why does suffering exist?*"

How does one appreciate happiness if they never had sadness to compare it to? How can someone be thankful for warmth if they've never experienced cold? How can one be grateful for life if they have never witnessed death? Every joy has a sadness meant to help us appreciate that what is good, and as Aquinas mentioned, all good is from God!

Throughout our life, we will inevitably be confronted with times of mourning. Whether it is a world disaster, a community catastrophe or a local tragedy, we can be happy in knowing that we are blessed to pass through the pain, just like Jesus did for us on the cross. Like Him, we will be defined by the amount of comfort we give to those who need us the most during their time of distress.

Without suffering, we might understand God's perfect love better, but we could never truly appreciate it.

13. Meekness

Blessed are the meek, for they shall inherit the earth.
- Matt. 5:5

---

14 St. Thomas Aquinas, *Aquinas's Shorter Summa* (Manchester, NH: Sophia Institute Press, 2003), Sec. 109

Dictionary.com defines the word meek as "showing patience and humility; gentle." The word tends to have a connotative interpretation. For most, to be "meek" tends to be a synonym for the word "weak."

The word "meek," however, takes on a whole new meaning when spoken by God. According to the *Navarre Study Bible*, "The meek are those who, imitating Christ, remain serene, humble and steadfast in adversity and do not give into bitterness or discouragement."[15] In other words, when defined theologically, the word "meek" denotes a heroic degree of perseverance, not weakness. That's why, when Jesus tells us "blessed are the meek, for they shall inherit the land," He doesn't mean that those with soft hearts will gain a bit of their father's acreage. He means that those with hearts strong enough will be co-heirs of heaven with Christ.

✝✝✝

We know through experience that the meek among us maintain a quiet, supernatural strength within them. We see it in our veteran teachers who have seasoned themselves with patience, gentleness, and humility throughout the years. We see it in our students when they choose to follow their consciences, even when everyone else is telling them to do otherwise. We see it inside of ourselves when we overcome the obstacles that keep us from becoming more like Christ.

Through practicing patience, gentleness and humility we provide a Christ-like example for our students to follow. Where they will follow us to is the indestructible power of God's glory.

Who could call that weak?

---

15 Navarre Study Bible Four Courts / Scepter; Expanded Edition (November 1, 2008)

14. Righteousness

Blessed are those who hunger and thirst for righteousness,
for they shall be satisfied.
- Matt. 5:6

Have you ever woke up late and didn't have time for break-fast? Left your water bottle or coffee mug at home? Skipped gro-cery shopping and had to live on oregano and cheese slices for a day? We've all been there and during these times our stomachs growl at us for ignoring them in such an indifferent way. As a result, our bellies send out a strong announcement throughout our bodies that doesn't secede until both hunger and thirst are nour-ished. Until they are satisfied, we aren't quite ourselves.

We hear Jesus announce the fifth beatitude in metaphor: *"Blessed are those who hunger and thirst for righteousness."* We've all been hungry and thirsty before, but just what does it mean to hunger and thirst for righteousness?

†††

When we are "righteous," we want only what is good and holy. In order to want what is good and holy, we must understand the source of all that is good and holy, namely God. The fifth be-atitude compares the physical act of eating and drinking to the spiritual act of submitting to God's will.

Just as our bodies need food and drink to feel physically complete, so do our souls need holiness to be spiritually complete. If we wish to satisfy our longing for holiness, we must follow through with our spiritual inclinations and answer His call within us to pray, act and serve. Only then will we truly be satisfied in faith.

When our stomachs rumble and our throats dry up, we are

automatically driven to satisfy our hunger and thirst. When we share a snack with our colleagues, our students and our communities, we are able to help them satisfy such hunger.

The question now is, what kinds of spiritual snacks are we sharing with them?

15. Mercy

Blessed are the merciful, for they shall obtain mercy.
- Matt. 5:7

"Nobody is perfect." We've heard this cliché phrase more times than we can count. Some people use it as an excuse for their shortcomings while others say it with a touch of humor that can ease the pressure off even the most precise perfectionist. Still, others refuse to accept the statement and find themselves searching for that which is perfect.

The sixth beatitude speaks of the mercy by which we can find perfection as sons and daughters of God. We do so by showing mercy.

By definition, mercy requires not only that we have an understanding of the shortcomings of others and ourselves, but that we forgive these imperfections and take the steps necessary to correct them. Mercy is the reason why Jesus sacrificed Himself for us: so that we could realize the wrong we do, ask His forgiveness, and commit ourselves to sin no more. When we accomplish these tasks, we discover the perfection we seek in the promise of His pardon.

††††

We are to practice mercy on a daily basis. This doesn't mean that we are to merely forgive our students' academic and spiritual shortcomings. On the contrary, it means that we should teach them first how to identify their weaknesses and second how to strengthen them. Every time we correct their work, call attention to their misbehavior, or encourage them to reach higher, we show them the mercy they need to become stronger students.

Jesus understood our sinful shortcomings and sacrificed Himself so that our sins could be forgiven. His suffering is made perfect only when we take the steps necessary to correct our errors. Our teaching becomes perfect when our students take the steps to correct their own academic and behavioral errors.

Through the practice of mercy, we discover that the phrase "Nobody is perfect" is false; for Jesus was, is and always will be perfect. His perfection dwells inside our learning environments, inside our students and inside of us.

So, what does that make us?

16. Purity

Blessed are the pure in heart, for they shall see God.
- Matt. 5:8

Our students are known for their innocence. Having not experienced the world in full, they come to us eager to learn about it. Through this curiosity, they humble themselves every time they sit in our presence and experience our lessons. The younger they are, the more we witness this virtue in practice.

Such innocence is what makes our job so wonderful. Although we surely have "adult duties," such as bills to pay, jobs to maintain, and schedules to keep, we find an oasis of innocence in the students we teach. In fact, every day we have an opportunity to see the world through the eyes of their purity. With such a lens to teach through, we sometimes find ourselves living our lives as if we were forever young.

†††

The seventh beatitude encourages us to live in this way by being "clean of heart" like the students we teach. To become like them, we must persevere in acquiring a clear conscience. This is not always easy, for it requires us to monitor ourselves not only in our external actions, but also in our interior motives.

Many people will turn old and grey before they experience the youthful sensation of attaining a clear conscience. I only hope that this never be the case for teachers, for we have the opportunity to cleanse our hearts and see God in every lesson we teach, every student we serve, and every virtue we model. When we attain this innocence, we become clean of heart and we can't help but see God in everything we do.

17. Peace

Blessed are the peacemakers, for they shall be called sons of God.
- Matt. 5:9

There is an often looked-over price that one pays when they decide to work for social justice. Jesus calls to mind the cost of becoming a peacemaker when He said, "Do you think that I have come to give peace on earth? No, I tell you, but rather division;"[16]

The cost for peace, then, is division. In other words, if we truly desire to work for peace and consequently be called children of God, our work must imitate Christ's and as a result, be a mani-

---

16 Luke 12:51

festation of His dividing spirit.

When we aspire for peace, we will encounter the rushing tide of the world and all of its evil temptations, but as Christ's children we will remain grounded in truth and guide the current of the worldly into the basin of Christ's love where it will remain tranquil for eternity.

†††

As teachers, we have the ability to stand firm against the current calamity that our society creates in each lesson we teach, through each student we motivate, and in every action that we commit. When we unify our efforts to the peaceful desires of God's will, we take on part of His identity and are rightly called children of God.

The rain will continue to come and the waters will rise up against our souls. What we do to protect our students from the temptations of sin will ultimately be the cornerstone of our spiritual work. When they are willing to join us in this battle, we will have successfully kept our Church out of harm's way, and given the Holy Spirit another outlet to enter into their lives.

18. Courage

Blessed are those who are persecuted for righteousness' sake, for theirs is the kingdom of heaven. Blessed are you when men revile you and persecute you and utter all kinds of evil against you falsely on my account. Rejoice and be glad, for your reward is great in heaven, for so men persecuted the prophets who were before you.
- Matt. 5:10-12

In this reading, Jesus specifically changes His wording to make this point clear; instead of saying "blessed are they" like in all of the other Beatitudes, He specifically states "blessed are you." This was done to inform us directly that if we wish to become part of the Kingdom, we will be insulted, persecuted and falsely accused of many evils.

This means that, because we live our faith through our teaching, we will find opposition, false presumptions, or even envy within our communities. It will be painful, but during these moments we must remember that we are blessed enough to go through them for God. As St. Paul reminds us, these sufferings make up for what is lacking in the afflictions of Christ Himself. [17] If we don't make this realization, there is a good chance that we might substitute our faith for fear.

✝✝✝

Throughout our careers, our minds will inevitably feel the tug of righteousness urging us to sprinkle the Gospel message into our practice. We will be tempted to pull back in order to satisfy the academic standards that our jobs require as opposed to allowing Christ to satisfy the spiritual standards that our missions mandate. Like Jesus before us, we must press on and allow His will to reign over all others, even if it means we must be persecuted in the process.

Blessed Archbishop Fulton J. Sheen's words bear the truth of this important message:

"The world will allow only the mediocre to live. It hates the very wicked, like the thieves [that hung at the sides of Christ], because they disturb its possessions and security. It also hates the Divinely Good, it hates our blessed Lord, because He disturbs its conscience, its heart, and its evil desires."[18]

---

17 1 Col. 24

18 Archbishop Fulton J. Sheen, *The Worlds' First Love Mary, Mother of God* (New York: McGraw-Hill Book Company, 1952)

19. Standards and Benchmarks

*He was praying in a certain place, and when he
ceased, one of his disciples said to him, "Lord, teach
us to pray, as John taught his disciples." And he said
to them, "When you pray, say:*

*"Father, hallowed be thy name.
Thy kingdom come.
Give us each day our daily bread;
and forgive us our sins, for we ourselves forgive every
one who is indebted to us;
and lead us not into temptation."*
- Luke 11:1-4

The Our Father, also known as the Lord's Prayer, is the only
prayer that Jesus taught to His disciples verbatim. We can imagine
that it was His hope that they would use it as a means to communicate themselves with their Father and establish a firm foundation for their spiritual growth. To this day, Christians recite these
words in hopes to follow in the footsteps of His first students.

This prayer is a marvel of linguistic construction. In this
prayer, as St. Thomas Aquinas wrote, "We ask, not only for all the
things we rightly desire, but also in the sequence that they should
be desired. This prayer teaches us not only to ask for things, but
also in what order we should desire them."[19]

That is why the prayer begins with the words "Our Father,"
and ends with the mention of evil and temptation, for we as a
unified community of believers should want His holy presence
among all other desires. When we complete the rest of the prayer,
we ask that God's will be done, that we be given what we need to
survive spiritually, and that we can continue in His presence even

---

19 St. Thomas Aquinas, *Summa Theologiae* II-II, 83, 9

after the words have been spoken. This is the standard by which we should pray.

†††

We have academic standards and benchmarks that our students must learn before passing on to the next grade. Like the Our Father, when we teach these guidelines word for word, we do well. However, we know that there are times when we need to go beyond the academic standards in order to ensure that our students learn. We also know that sometimes, a regular conversation with God can touch our souls in a way the Our Father can't.

The truth is, both are needed. Academic standards need the creative extensions that we give them in order to breathe life into our students' curiosity. So too, does the Our Father need the spiritual extensions that the Holy Spirit gives us in order to breathe life into His people.

Use both as skeletons before preparing your instruction. Then, add meat.

20. Rules

But I say to you that hear, Love your enemies, do good to those who hate you, bless those who curse you, pray for those who abuse you. To him who strikes you on the cheek, offer the other also; and from him who takes away your coat do not withhold even your shirt. Give to everyone who begs from you; and of him who takes away your goods do not ask them again. And as you wish that men would do to you, do so to them.
- Luke 6:27-31

Strict rule enforcement is critical to the survival of any community, especially our learning environments. Effective teachers know that there are two ways to do this: through fear, or through hope.

Where strict rule enforcement exists in our world, people tend to be motivated to comply to the rules because they fear the consequences that will happen if they don't: We don't rob banks because we fear we'll land ourselves in jail. We don't drive 100 miles per hour on a street that has a 25 mile per hour speed limit because we fear a police officer will be waiting around the corner. These fearful consequences are just a few that can be compared to how the Jewish people of the Old Testament felt every time they sinned and their consequence was "an eye for an eye," or retaliation and repayment for the crime committed.

†††

However, Christ shows us a new way to look at strict rule enforcement. It is the way of hope. When we are motivated to do the right thing because it is good, not because we fear the consequences, we solidify our hopeful desires with God. This way is fearless, because we are constantly moved to do virtuous acts that help build His Kingdom, regardless of what the consequences might be.

Our Father has very high expectations for us; He wants us to earn eternal life with Him in heaven. To complete this task, He has established strict rules by which we are to abide by while on earth. Some follow these rules because they fear going to Hell. Others follow them fearlessly because they are in hope of Heaven. The latter see fear as a filial means by which they can please their celestial Father through their obedience.

Why do your students follow your rules?

21. Thought

When you give alms, do not let your left hand know what your right hand is doing... But when you pray, go into your room and shut the door and pray to your Father who is in secret; and your Father who sees in secret will reward you.
- Matt. 6:3, 6

Our brain is a magnificent specimen. It has the power to simultaneously store, recall, organize and even create information through various physiological connections. It can balance our artistic and mathematical knowledge, automatically run our bodily functions, and create within us our very personalities. It is truly a work of art; the quintessential masterpiece of the human body.

St. Matthew pays tribute to the Creator of this holy phenomenon and reminds us how close we are connected to God because of it. For thought, as we know it, is nothing more than an effect of His original invention of the mind. Every contemplation we have goes forth from the mind and ends with its original inventor. That's why it is safe to say that every thought we make, good or bad, is a prayer that we send to our all-knowing Lord.

††††

For that reason, it is important that we guide our thoughts towards that which is good, true and beautiful. When we unify our thoughts perpetually towards the will of God, we learn how to habitually recognize His presence in all that we see. When we succeed in this practice, we unite our souls to His celestial body and allow ourselves to further construct His Church within the learning environments we are commissioned to teach in.

The mission of any school in the world is to nurture the progression of the mind. As Christian teachers, we recognize that the main ingredient to this recipe is thought, which is not owned by the district, the school, the teacher, nor the students themselves. It is owned by God, who already knows our prayer before we think it.

We are always praying because we are always thinking.

22. The Point of No Return

As they were going along the road, a man said to him, "I will follow you wherever you go." And Jesus said to him, "Foxes have holes, and birds of the air have nests; but the Son of man has nowhere to lay his head." To another he said, "Follow me." But he said, "Lord, let me first go and bury my father." But he said to him, "Leave the dead to bury their own dead; but as for you, go and proclaim the kingdom of God." Another said, "I will follow you, Lord; but let me first say farewell to those at my home." Jesus said to him, "No one who puts his hand to the plow and looks back is fit for the kingdom of God."
- Luke 9:57-62

Think about the hardest class you have ever taken. Take an extra minute and think about what was required of you in order to pass it. Were there several essays? A tremendously difficult final exam? A project that required more time than you actually had? All of the above?

Now, think about your teacher for that class. Did he have clear expectations? Did he check in on your progress often? Did he encourage you by making the seemingly difficult tasks seem possible through his instruction? Or, did he merely have unrealistic expectations?

Jesus had unrealistic expectations. In this reading, you can see that His requirements wouldn't allow for the means, time nor energy for the man to bury his father. Jesus wanted him to follow Him and he wanted it now.

†††

In education, we graduate our students and move them along the road towards academic success. We do this by raising the academic rigor much like Jesus did with the man in this reading, so that they will be prepared for their future. In raising the bar, they reach higher to grow in intellect and understanding.

For Christian teachers, we must make it very clear that our expectations go beyond those that our grade level mandates. Especially towards the middle and end of the year, we must set the bar higher than expected so that they will understand what it will take for them to succeed in their future education.

Jesus made it very clear to His students that if they followed Him, they would need to give up their comfort and work very hard to earn the merits of discipleship. We must recognize this "point of no return" in our own spirituality and mimic its value inside our learning environments by encouraging our students to step outside of their comfort zones...often. We do this when we raise the rigor to the next level.

If we do this academically, our students will easily survive in their next grade. When we do this spiritually, they will happily live in eternal life.

23. Guaranteed Success

Now the parable is this: The seed is the word of God.
The ones along the path are those who have heard;

then the devil comes and takes away the word from their hearts, that they may not believe and be saved. And the ones on the rock are those who, when they hear the word, receive it with joy; but these have no root, they believe for a while and in time of temptation fall away. And as for what fell among the thorns, they are those who hear, but as they go on their way they are choked by the cares and riches and pleasures of life, and their fruit does not mature. And as for that in the good soil, they are those who, hearing the word, hold it fast in an honest and good heart, and bring forth fruit with patience.
- Luke 8:11-15

Teachers share a certain love for servitude with Jesus. We experience hardships and sacrifice on a daily basis so that our students will at the very least have a chance to succeed. We do all we can to lead them to water, but the truth is, we cannot make them drink.

But there is good news! Jesus speaks about how His Kingdom will be a guaranteed success. He first described the failures of some who will be like the scorched seeds and the seeds caught in the thorns. But then he mentioned the seeds that will fall on good soil and produce a hundred or sixty or thirtyfold. The message of these descriptions is clear: there will be losses in those who oppose His teachings, but there will be many more gains.

†††

These gains will come through education. As God's field workers, it is our job to sow the seeds of our students' intellects and plant them in the soil of truth. It is then up to God to provide the nutrients they need to help them grow and produce a hundred or sixty or thirtyfold. In other words, it is up to us to teach effectively, to plant the seed, but it is up to Him to open their hearts to our lessons and make them grow.

Mother Teresa once said that "God does not demand that I be successful. God demands that I be faithful."[20] This means that whether or not we do our job, He will surely do His. Guaranteed success is the promise He gives us if we remain faithful to our vocations.

24. Mystery

They went on from there and passed through Galilee. And he would not have any one know it; for he was teaching his disciples, saying to them, "The Son of man will be delivered into the hands of men, and they will kill him; and when he is killed, after three days he will rise."
- Mark 9:30-31

The disciples continued to walk with Jesus to Galilee but not as confidently as before. Jesus' prediction about His death and resurrection confused and troubled them. They were so weakened by His words they were afraid to question Him.

Jesus had a knack for humbling people by challenging them to think for themselves. In this instance, He made His disciples think about life without His physical presence so as to prepare them for the day He would go home to the Father. We can be sure that His followers thought profoundly about what these words meant until they came to understand them fully on the day of Christ's resurrection.

We try to be as clear as possible when giving tasks for our

---

20 José Luís Gonzalez-Balado, *In My Own Words: The Sayings of Mother Teresa* (Liguori, MO: Liguori Publications,1997)

students to complete. But sometimes, it is the mystery of the unknown that motivates them to think deeply like the disciples. We should imitate this teaching style of Jesus and propose a mystery that our students must ponder to achieve success. We'll be surprised to see how quickly our class will unite in interest through this methodology.

In its essence, faith is a mystery that will forever go unproven by scientific standards. For that reason, we as Christians are enamored by the truth we find within our faith. If we can teach our students to appreciate the mysteries our teachings have to offer, we can create a gateway for the Holy Spirit to reveal to them the mysterious truths that our faith entails.

His Teaching Methods

The word "teach" has its roots in the Latin relation of the word "token." If we look at the French and Spanish words for teach, "enseigner" and "enseñar," we notice the word "sign" embedded within each. Brother William Harkens, FSC noted it best when he wrote that, "To teach is to decipher signs, to show some token of the richer, fuller meaning of what is at hand."[21]

This section is a tool that teachers and parents from every walk of life can use to enlighten our students with the "richer and fuller meaning" of life. It provides a brief and deep journey through the Gospels with the master Teacher, Jesus of Nazareth, who shares His best teaching secrets with you along the way. Take notes, because there is a test (but it won't start until after you die).

25. Storytelling

And he called them to him, and said to them in parables.
- Mark 3: 23

---

21 Br. William Harkins, FSC, Keynote address: *Teacher as Minister: Signs and Metaphors*, (20-22 Apr. 1988), at http://db.cbconf.org

Jesus' use of parables made people think about much more than the mere comprehension of worldly ideals. His parables put the responsibility of understanding truth on the learner, so that it was not a direct statement of truth from Him, the teacher. These stories allowed His students to open the doors of their hearts and to ponder what was said.

We too should follow Jesus' example and create our own modern day parables. To better craft our storytelling abilities, it is important that we look at the foundations of Jesus' stories so as to build upon His work. Almost all of His parables included the following:

- They were popular and easily comprehended for the most part.
- They were entertaining and realistic.
- Each story contained a hidden spiritual message that, when presented to the intellect, could be contemplated, accepted, or refuted by the individual person.

†††

Tell stories! Use your past experiences as your primary source. They give you credibility. If you do not have many experiences, research people who do and retell their story. If all else fails, make up a story. Nothing can capture a child's attention better than a good story as told by someone they love.

To teach like Jesus, we must not allow ourselves to "give" the answers to our students. Rather, we should give them just enough logical information to contemplate and enough unanswered questions to base their decisions on their faith. Parables and stories are a great way to do this.

26. Reflecting

And in the morning, a great while before day, he rose and went out to a lonely place, and there he prayed. And Simon and those who were with him pursued him, and they found him and said to him, "Every one is searching for you." And he said to them, "Let us go on to the next towns, that I may preach there also; for that is why I came out." And he went throughout all Galilee, preaching in their synagogues and casting out demons.
- Mark 1:35-39

This reading offers a slight inference to what was on Jesus' mind during His secluded prayer time. Once found by His disciples, He told them, "Let us go into the nearby villages so I may preach there also. For this purpose I have come." This comment to His disciples makes it clear that Jesus, during His time with His Father in prayer, was reflecting on His purpose.

†††

As teachers, it is of the greatest importance that we reflect frequently on the purpose we have been given. God might work through our students, colleagues, and community to teach us a lesson, but these lessons cannot be understood if we do not review them with the greatest teacher of all time, Jesus. In conferencing with Him in silent prayer, He gives us what we need in order to teach effectively.

Reflection is also important on the academic level. It is vital that we take time after each day, week, semester and year to reflect on the teaching methods we have used to help our students learn. In essence, our teaching style should be a lump of never-drying clay that can be molded into shape at any given time through holy contemplation.

To reflect on our past lessons and future purpose gives Jesus the opportunity to develop us into the teacher He wants, so that our students can be sculpted by His molding hands as well.

"We are the clay, and thou art our potter;"[22]

27. Teaching "To the Point"

He did not speak to them without a parable, but privately to his own disciples he explained everything.
- Mark 4:34

We can identify with Jesus in that it is not always the best option to speak only in clever parables because the whole message might get lost in translation. At times, it is necessary to "get to the point," so to speak, and "explain everything to our students in private."

Winston Churchill, famous British Prime Minister during World War II and former member of the Church of England, understood this concept very well when he made the following statement:

"If you have an important point to make, don't try to be subtle or clever. Use the pile driver. Hit the point once. Then come back and hit it again. Then hit it a third time; a tremendous whack."

†††

Jesus gave His students ample description of the Kingdom of heaven in His numerous parables. He even went a step further and individualized and explained their meaning to His closest fol-

---

22 Isa. 64:8

lowers. His students were exposed to His message of the kingdom so often that misunderstanding it would have been almost impossible.

That is why we too should teach in a creative manner that leaves no room for error in understanding on our students' part. It would do us good to reinforce our lessons as often as needed so that our students will grasp the ideas we attempt to teach them.

Just like Moses was attracted to the burning bush and Saul was thrown to the ground on the way to Damascus, sometimes the most direct message is the clearest.

Jab with clarity. Save the knock-out punch of parables for the next round.

28. Keeping It Simple

And when Jesus saw their faith, he said to the paralytic, "My son, your sins are forgiven." Now some of the scribes were sitting there, questioning in their hearts, "Why does this man speak thus? It is blasphemy! Who can forgive sins but God alone?"
And immediately Jesus, perceiving in his spirit that they thus questioned within themselves, said to them, "Why do you question thus in your hearts? Which is easier, to say to the paralytic, 'Your sins are forgiven,' or to say, 'Rise, take up your pallet and walk?' But that you may know that the Son of man has authority on earth to forgive sins"– he said to the paralytic – "I say to you, rise, take up your pallet and go home." And he rose, and immediately took up the pallet and went out before them all; so that they were all amazed and glorified God, saying, "We never saw anything like this!"
- Mark 2:5-12

The paralytic man in this reading was much like the leper that Jesus healed in chapter one of Mark's Gospel. People believed that he was being punished with leprosy as punishment for his past sins. In fighting against their sneers, he truly believed that Jesus would heal him physically. What he probably didn't count on was being healed *spiritually.*

Jesus began the healing by saying, "your sins are forgiven" for a reason. For Him, this was the simplest way to teach His students, especially the one being healed, that He was given the power to heal sinful souls *and* to heal suffering bodies. One of these healings was more important than the other, which is why Jesus refers to it in His first words to the paralytic man.

†††

Human beings have been attempting to make the simple world a more confusing place. Jesus teaches us that we must eliminate confusion when possible and keep it simple. Just as Jesus turned the attention from the paralytic's fading physical body to the everlasting spirit that dwelled within him, so we should steer our lessons from the curriculum towards that which will speak to our students' souls.

We might not know how to teach in this way just yet. When we consult our Lord through silent prayer and active teaching, we can be sure that He will give us the grace necessary to do His work correctly.

"When the answer is simple, God is speaking"

~Albert Einstein

29. On Being Serious

And immediately there was in their synagogue a man

*with an unclean spirit; and he cried out, "What have
you to do with us, Jesus of Nazareth? Have you come to
destroy us? I know who you are, the Holy One of God."
But Jesus rebuked him, saying, "Be silent, and come
out of him!" And the unclean spirit, convulsing him
and crying with a loud voice, came out of him. And they
were all amazed, so that they questioned among themselves, saying, "What is this? A new teaching! With authority he commands even the unclean spirits, and they
obey him." And at once his fame spread everywhere
throughout all the surrounding region of Galilee.*
- Mark 1:23-28

Unclean spirits are as easy to find today as they were in the
time of Jesus. In Jesus' day, we find one inside the holiest of places, the local Jewish synagogue. Recognizing the creator that he
turned his back on a long time ago, this evil spirit heckled Jesus.
Jesus could have easily ignored the man or showed him the greatest amount of kindness in the world, but Jesus had an appropriate
response in mind. This situation required a certain degree of seriousness.

We sometimes get caught up in the idea that we must portray
a very "kind" image for ourselves, our students and our educational community. Although it is completely necessary that we do
show kindness and that we do so often, there is a great danger in
"overdoing it."

In a commentary on C.S. Lewis' book, *The Problem of Pain*,
Jacek Bacz wrote the following to illustrate this point.

*God's idea of goodness is almost certainly unlike ours; yet,
God's moral judgment must differ from ours. Thus, where God
means Love, we only mean Kindness, "the desire to see others
than self happy; not happy in this way or in that, but just happy."
We want "not so much a Father but a grandfather in heaven,"*

a God "who said of anything we happened to like doing, 'What does it matter so long as they are contented?'" But Love is not mere Kindness. "Kindness cares not whether its object becomes good or bad, provided only that it escapes suffering", while Love "would rather see (the loved ones) suffer much than be happy in contemptible and estranging modes."[23]

†††

Sometimes we tend to replace the professional relationship that our community needs with a friendly relationship that our community *wants*. Many times we choose to "entertain" instead of teach which, in the long run, provides very little benefit to our students and colleagues.

Jesus understood the benefits of being both professional and friendly at the same time. He was kind at all times and yet still used the gift of seriousness frequently. He was very strict, but also very fair. For that reason, all of His students understood His love; even the demons!

30. Responding to "I Don't Get It."

And when he was alone, those who were about him with the twelve asked him concerning the parables. And he said to them, "To you has been given the secret of the kingdom of God, but for those outside everything is in parables; so that they may indeed see but not perceive, and may indeed hear but not understand; lest they should turn again, and be forgiven." And he said to them, "Do you not understand this parable? How

---

23 Jacek Bacz. "C.S. Lewis: The Problem of Pain." *The Newman Rambler* (1999) at http://www.evangelizationstation.com

then will you understand all the parables?"
- Mark 4:10-13

Jesus' disciples "questioned him about the parables." Notice how St. Mark makes no mention of the specific questions they asked. Jesus' students did what the majority of our students do every day when they don't understand something: they approach their teacher and make a general statement like, "I don't get it."

This phrase tends to get under our skin a bit more than people of any other profession. It usually lets us know that either we didn't do a good enough job of teaching the material or our students didn't do a good enough job of learning it. The truth is it is usually a mix of both.

†††

In Jesus' case, He is the perfect teacher, so we can assume that it was a misunderstanding on His students' part that led them to ask Him questions. To respond to their doubts, He said, "Do you not understand this parable? Then how will you understand any of the parables?" By saying this, He refused to accept "I don't get it," from His students and demanded that they take more responsibility in their learning.

When we succeed in making our students think in this way, we allow the Holy Spirit to work in their hearts through questioning. Like the disciples, there will be a time when our students will come to Jesus and say, "I don't get it." This is when the Holy Spirit will guide them to dig deeper into their faith and to find the answers to the questions that burn within their hearts.

We should always be available to help them find these answers.

31. Using Synonyms

And he said to them, "Is a lamp brought in to be put under a bushel, or under a bed, and not on a stand? For there is nothing hid, except to be made manifest; nor is anything secret, except to come to light. If any man has ears to hear, let him hear."
- Mark 4:21-23

There are several names for our God: Father, Abba, Alpha and Omega, Son, Christ, Jesus, Savior, Redeemer, Holy Spirit, and Trinity are just a few. These words identify the One Being that we believe created the world. Would it not be logical, then, to identify this same God through His creations? In other words, could we call God love, kindness, mercy, justice, and faith?

Jesus tells us that "there is nothing hidden except to be made visible; nothing secret except to come to light." This means that one day, every human being will come to a complete understanding of the Gospel message that Jesus has mandated us to teach. Whether it is in this life or the next, Jesus will not allow any of His children to go without knowing the truth that will eventually set them free.

††††

As teachers armed with the realization of this truth, we find it impossible to keep Jesus out of our lessons because everything we teach has its point of origin in Him. Through God's creations, we find an infinite amount of synonyms by which we are able to recognize God. These words pave the way for the Gospel to be spread in our learning environments.

In the words of C.S. Lewis, "I believe in Christianity as I believe that the sun has risen: not only because I see it, but because by it I see everything else."[24] The synonyms of Jesus are as limitless as His creations. May we recognize them in every lesson we teach.

32. Organizing and Cleaning

While he was in one of the cities, there came a man full of leprosy; and when he saw Jesus, he fell on his face and besought him, "Lord, if you will, you can make me clean." And he stretched out his hand, and touched him, saying, "I will; be clean." And immediately the leprosy left him. And he charged him to tell no one; but "go and show yourself to the priest, and make an offering for your cleansing, as Moses commanded, for a proof to the people." But so much the more the report went abroad concerning him; and great multitudes gathered to hear and to be healed of their infirmities. But he withdrew to the wilderness and prayed.
- Luke 5:12-16

Teachers have a lot on their plates. Since we bounce from class to class, paper to paper, test to test, and meeting to meeting, we find ourselves with little time and a lot of work. Homeschooling teachers aren't much better. They have tasks to complete at home, jobs to complete and students to teach. During the short hours we spend in our learning environments, the amount of work can pile so high that sometimes we forget we have a desk as it lay beneath a pile of memorandums, student work, or teaching materials.

Students also have difficulty organizing and cleaning. Their material piles are sometimes more of a disaster than ours. Al-

---

24 C.S. Lewis, "Is Theology Poetry?" *They Asked for a Paper* (1962). (Reprinted by Samizdat, 2014)

though the items that topple off and on of Mount Messy might be different than ours, the truth of the matter is that some of our students are just as busy as us, if not more. The ones who are not organized enough to keep up with their own busy schedules tend to suffer the most.

†††

St. Luke focuses on the healing of a leper by the miraculous action of Jesus. Of course, we've seen Jesus heal many people through each of the Gospels, but the words that the leper uses to request Jesus' mercy signify just how faithful he was: "Lord, if You wish, You can make me clean."

As we look at the pile of messiness that builds upon our desks, within our students' areas, and anywhere else in our learning environments, perhaps we can be like the leper by showing our faith through our cleanliness and order. When we tidy up our unorganized and grubby spaces, may we see these actions as a means for spiritual renewal and pray "Lord, if You wish, You can make me clean too."

33. Building Vocabulary

That evening they brought to him many who were possessed with demons; and he cast out the spirits with a word, and healed all who were sick. This was to fulfill what was spoken by the prophet Isaiah, "He took our infirmities and bore our diseases."
- Matt. 8:16-17

In the world of language, words vary in their degree of use and importance. The word "red" for example, comes up so often both in sight and sound that we very rarely misinterpret its meaning. When the word "divide" comes up we figure out how to successfully complete the mathematical process of division. The word "munificent" might have never crossed our path and it is very probable that most of us do not know what it means, yet it still exists for a purpose.

Jesus "drove out the spirits with a word" (italics added). He didn't touch the sick. He didn't rattle off a long speech to rid them of their demons. He didn't even fast for weeks beforehand. Rather, He spoke only a word to save them.

†††

In our learning environments, we follow this teaching strategy every time we introduce a new vocabulary word to our students. We stress their importance and use them repeatedly until we feel our students have understood enough to use them correctly in speech and in their written work. When they have truly learned these words, they are able to convey meaning with them and through them.

As Taoist philosopher Cuang Tzu stated, "The purpose of a rabbit snare is to catch a rabbit and once the rabbit is caught, the snare is forgotten. The purpose of a Word is to convey ideas. Once the ideas are grasped, the words are forgotten."[25] A good teacher should always remember there is great power in every word: that power is the Holy Spirit, who created the ideas and objects that our simple languages attempt to communicate through Education.

(By the way, according to dictionary.com, the word "munificent" means: extremely liberal in giving; very generous.)

---

25 Cuang Tzu, *The Way of Cuang Tzu* (1965), (Reprinted, Boston: Shambhala, 2004)

34. Experiencing Learning

And he went up on the mountain, and called to him those whom he desired; and they came to him. And he appointed twelve, to be with him, and to be sent out to preach and have authority to cast out demons: Simon whom he surnamed Peter; James the son of Zebedee and John the brother of James, whom he surnamed Bo-anerges, that is, sons of thunder; Andrew, and Philip, and Bartholomew, and Matthew, and Thomas, and James the son of Alphaeus, and Thaddaeus, and Simon the Cananaean, and Judas Iscariot, who betrayed him. Then he went home.
- Mark 3:13-19

Jesus knew that if His disciples didn't experience the life-giving power that He was offering to them, they would never truly understand the Gospel message that He would later trust them to spread after His death and resurrection. He appointed them as apostles in this reading so that they could learn by *doing* what He commanded them, not just by following Him.

This is one of the best practices we as teachers can offer our own students – allowing them to *experience* learning by actually participating in it. Confucius explained this message very well when he said, "Tell me; and I will forget. Show me; and I will remember. Involve me; and I will understand forever."[26] (Confucius wasn't even Christian and yet, still evokes great Christian values in some of his maxims.)

†††

Our students have been "appointed" to us by Jesus Himself.

---

26 Confucius, *The Sayings of Confucius* (Reprinted, Gloucestershire, England: Echo Library, 2008)

He has "summoned those who He wanted" to be sitting in the desks that face us every day. Like Him, we should first give them the example to follow in ourselves so that they can remember. Then, we should allow them to experience their own learning even if they have to suffer a bit. When they practice what we preach, they will then understand forever.

Just as we appoint our students to involve themselves in their own learning, so we are appointed by God to be His light for those in darkness. To apply the message of this Gospel message, we too must accept God's call within us to act on His behalf. We are His present day disciples, and it is up to us to teach our students the way to eternal life.

35. Adding a Touch of Crazy

And when his family heard it, they went out to seize him, for people were saying, "He is beside himself."
- Mark 3:21

C.S. Lewis, former atheist and convert to the Church of England, wrote in his book, *Mere Christianity*, a great defense in response to the Scribes during the time of Jesus that still holds true for us today. He wrote:

"You must make your choice. Either this man was, and is, the son of God: or else a madman or something worse… You can shut Him up for a fool, you can spit at Him and kill Him as a demon; or you can fall at His feet and call Him Lord and God. But let us not come up with any patronizing nonsense about His being a great human teacher. He has not left that open to us. He did not intend to."[27]

---

27 C.S. Lewis, *Mere Christianity* (Beach Centre, Singapore: C.S. Lewis Pte. Ltd., 1952)

In his argument, Lewis reveals Jesus to be one of three things: a liar, a lunatic, or the Lord. He argues that if we accept Him as merely a "great moral teacher," and not the Lord He claimed to be, we would be in the wrong. He needed to be both, for no person who is a lunatic can be "a great moral teacher." No one who is a liar can be a "great moral teacher" either. In fact, there is no one who would be willing to be put to death in the way Jesus was for a lie. If that were the case, then He would be out of His mind.

The only logical conclusion we can make is that Jesus was, in fact, the Lord that he claimed to be. Being the Lord is the only way He could have been a "great moral teacher," for He would have had the Spirit of God running through His veins to guide Him.

†††

As educators, we too are given the same Spirit to guide us into becoming "great moral teachers." St. Mark invites us to embrace the madness of our profession and justify it by the fact that God Has willed it to be so. The actions of Jesus were considered crazy by His people, even His own relatives! Some of our tactics and techniques might seem nutty or ludicrous, but sometimes the unorthodox can be used effectively in teaching those nearest to us.

We must always be able to respond to our scribes that our work is pure and willed by God. If it is not, then we are merely liars and lunatics.

36. Teaching with the Five (or Six) Senses

And as Jesus passed on from there, two blind men followed him, crying aloud, "Have mercy on us, Son of David." When he entered the house, the blind men

came to him; and Jesus said to them, "Do you believe that I am able to do this?" They said to him, "Yes, Lord." Then he touched their eyes, saying, "According to your faith be it done to you." And their eyes were opened. And Jesus sternly charged them, "See that no one knows it."But they went away and spread his fame through all that district.
- Matt. 9:27-31

Of the five senses, sight, hearing, smell, taste and touch, which would be the one you would least like to lose? Many of us would respond by saying, "I wouldn't want to lose ANY of them!"

Our senses are both blessings and curses. With them, we are able to experience the fresh smell of the morning as well as the sometimes offensive odor of adolescent youth. We can taste the freshness of recently picked fruit and vegetables and spit out the bitterness of a burnt kernel of popcorn. Indeed, all of our senses help us experience both the good and the bad this world has to offer.

†††

But there is one sense that is missing – a spiritual sense that God gives to all of His children. This "sixth sense" is our intellectual capacity to know, love and serve God. This sense is by far the most important because it works with the others to bring out the deeper, fuller meaning of what we experience.

For example, Jesus heals two men of their physical blindness as a means to penetrate their spiritual 'sixth' senses. The miraculous healing was not committed so that everyone would come to know Jesus' power, rather, it happened because He wanted to open the men's eyes to the wonders of the world that could only be appreciated by knowing God first. In essence, it took physical vision to see spiritual truth in Him.

While we prepare our lessons, it would do us well to imitate Christ's example and utilize the five carnal senses as a means to help our students understand the necessity of knowing, loving and serving God. When we join these lessons with our Christian faith and zeal, they are sure to become effective, memorable, and truly meaningful.

37. Guiding Conversations

Then a blind and dumb demoniac was brought to him, and he healed him, so that the dumb man spoke and saw. And all the people were amazed, and said, "Can this be the Son of David?" But when the Pharisees heard it they said, "It is only by Be-elzebul, the prince of demons, that this man casts out demons." Knowing their thoughts, he said to them, "Every kingdom divided against itself is laid waste, and no city or house divided against itself will stand; and if Satan casts out Satan, he is divided against himself; how then will his kingdom stand? And if I cast out demons by Be-elzebul, by whom do your sons cast them out? Therefore they shall be your judges. But if it is by the Spirit of God that I cast out demons, then the kingdom of God has come upon you."
- Matt. 12:22-28

When people gather into groups for whatever reason, a certain dichotomy of thought and speech exists. When people speak, they attempt to express their thoughts successfully to others. While they listen, they attempt to make sense of what has been said. When the words spoken cause people to think deeply, and then respond with more thought provoking words, this is when quality conversation occurs.

As educators, we know that academic conversations can do one of two things – they can elaborate on our lessons successfully, or they can utterly confuse our students. The deciding factor between these two extremes is how well we guide the conversation into prosperity.

Jesus showed us how to do this successfully. The conversation began with a thought provoking question; "Could this perhaps be the Son of David?" As the people were pondering this glorious possibility, the Pharisees gave their own opinion of the matter and as a result, confused the people into believing a lie. Jesus recognized the path that the conversation was taking, and then turned it back onto the right path.

†††

When we use the teaching tactic of leading group conversations with our students, questions, doubts, misconceptions, and tangents will surely arise just as they did in Jesus' experiences. When this happens, we must be ready to respond with the truth and clarity that our students need to get the most out of the conversation as it deals with the lessons being taught. Freedom to express their thoughts must be present, but limitations on these freedoms should also exist to ensure that proper understanding is achieved.

In the ocean of education the crashing waves are the words our students express, and the depth of the water is their profound capacity for thought. Whether the seas are calm or a tidal wave is on the rise, may we be the steadfast anchors that ground our classroom conversations in truth.

38. Using New Media

And when they had crossed over, they came to land at Gennesaret, and moored to the shore. And when they got out of the boat, immediately the people recognized him, and ran about the whole neighborhood and began to bring sick people on their pallets to any place where they heard he was. And wherever he came, in villages, cities, or country, they laid the sick in the market places, and besought him that they might touch even the fringe of his garment; and as many as touched it were made well.
- Mark 6:53-56

I remember back when I was in elementary school my teachers would celebrate our accomplishments by tacking our 100% spelling tests to a cork bulletin board in the hallway outside of our classroom. I remember feeling proud of myself every time my name was there, found precariously between a large yellow tack and the words "Good job!" written in red ink just beside it. This is an example of my teachers using "old media" to allow others to affirm my success.

In today's age some people continue this practice. They hang student projects from the ceiling and tape reports to the wall. It is always a joy to walk into an elementary classroom or homeschooling household because it is always swimming with student creativity and color.

Another group of teachers is taking it a step further. While continuing the use of traditional "Old Media," they are extending their practice to their students (and beyond) through the use of "New Media." New Media and Old Media can be defined in the following ways:

Old Media: A one-way mode of communication where the principle communicator is in control of the message being delivered. The receiver is able to accept it as fact or opinion. Examples include television, radio, and postal mail.

New Media: A two-way mode of communication where the essential message is compacted by one person, but the receiver is able to engage themselves as well. Both parties are able to share opinions and reasoning through a flow of rich discussion. Examples include YouTube, Facebook, Twitter, Tumblr, blogs etc.

††††

In order to proclaim His healing message to all, Jesus used the one link that both Old and New Media need to survive: word of mouth. In a sense, the people of Gennesaret went viral with Jesus' message and because of that, several people came to know and love Him.

In our learning environments, we must imitate Jesus' way and go "viral" with His messages through the use of both Old and New Media. When we are able to showcase our students' accomplishments both inside our learning environments and online through blogs, videos and other digital means, their sense of pride will multiply and our hopes for spreading the Gospel message within their souls will spread like wildfire to the souls of the millions that inhabit the digital world.

39. Making a Name for Yourself

And Jesus went on from there and passed along the Sea of Galilee. And he went up on the mountain, and sat down there. And great crowds came to him, bringing

*with them the lame, the maimed, the blind, the dumb,
and many others, and they put them at his feet, and he
healed them, so that the throng wondered, when they
saw the dumb speaking, the maimed whole, the lame
walking, and the blind seeing; and they glorified the
God of Israel.*
- Matt. 15:29-31

Jesus is arguably the most well-known figure in history.
From the wealthy to the impoverished, Jesus sets His salvific precepts into the hearts of every man and woman. People of all races,
cultures, denominations and continents are at some point in their
lives struck by the immense effect that the Son of Man had on
mankind.

We find this same striking effect written on the pages of Matthew's Gospel and all over the faces of those who watched Jesus
act. The evangelist tells us that they were "amazed" at what they
saw and because of their amazement, they intuitively "glorified to
God of Israel." This glorification combined with amazement is exactly the effect that the Gospel message has on people; Over two
thousand years the effect continues to ripple through our souls.

†††

Our present-day culture describes such a fanatic following as
the posse of a rockstar. People congregated around Jesus in much
the same way people surround popular music artists, singing their
every lyric as if they were part of a duet with the lead. They travel
to their concerts through the constant rhythm that beats in their
head, following each note to the stage so that they too might believe and praise the musical talents of their heroes.

Jesus, a politically powerless carpenter's son from a town in
the middle of nowhere during the time of the Roman empire, was

more popular than a rockstar. You, an underpaid and overworked crux of imagination and will, will be well known for your charity as long as you allow yourself to be like Him. When we provide our students with constant and authentic examples of Christian virtue in the learning environment, they will congregate around us, recall our every lesson and continue the ripple that began in our souls over 2,000 years ago.

40. Getting Frustrated

On the next day, when they had come down from the mountain, a great crowd met him. And behold, a man from the crowd cried, "Teacher, I beg you to look upon my son, for he is my only child; and behold, a spirit seizes him, and he suddenly cries out; it convulses him till he foams, and shatters him, and will hardly leave him. And I begged your disciples to cast it out, but they could not." Jesus answered, "O faithless and perverse generation, how long am I to be with you and bear with you? Bring your son here." While he was coming, the demon tore him and convulsed him. But Jesus rebuked the unclean spirit, and healed the boy, and gave him back to his father. And all were astonished at the majesty of God. But while they were all marveling at everything he did, he said to his disciples.
- Luke 9:37-43

Teachers have mile-long lists of reasons to be frustrated: underachieving students, missing materials, schedule changes, late homework, and the list could go on. Frustration is so much a part of our lives that we rarely stop to think about it.

However, frustration is one of those feelings that can be beneficial to our spiritual health. For example, take a look at Jesus. He was beyond frustrated at the poor man and even ridiculed His students openly about it. His frustration translated into a miracle that not only saved a small boy's life, but also guided others towards the correct path.

†††

We typically see frustration as a bitter drink that every store in the spiritual realm offers at a cheap price. It requires less self-control and endurance and, because it asks so little of us, it enters into our systems in troughs and becomes addictive. For that reason, we tend to see it as a distraction to our spiritual perfection.

St. Luke shows us that the contrary is true. Granted, we all have a limit to the amount of frustration we can handle, but like a nice glass of wine taken in moderation, frustration can enter our spiritual diet and make it healthier, stronger, and more pure...just like the boy Jesus healed.

41. Forcing It

When evening came, his disciples went down to the sea, got into a boat, and started across the sea to Caper-na-um. It was now dark, and Jesus had not yet come to them. The sea rose because a strong wind was blowing. When they had rowed about three or four miles, they saw Jesus walking on the sea and drawing near to the boat. They were frightened, but he said to them, "It is I; do not be afraid." Then they were glad to take him into the boat, and immediately the boat was at the land to which they were going.
- John 6:16-21

Differentiation is one of the educator's most important teaching tools, but at the same time it can also be our worst enemy. Based on the Christian doctrine of free will, we use choice as a healthy motivator for students who are mature enough to handle it, but cringe at the fact that we are unable to offer it to those who are still irresponsible learners. The fact that we are not able to provide each student with educational free will drives us nuts.

Jesus must have felt the same way. His disciples were struggling to comprehend His divinity, so as a lesson to them all He made them get into the boat to go before Him. There was no option, He literally forced them to follow His required instructions. In other words, He did not differentiate this lesson for them.

As a result, they suffered in the midst of periling danger, were saved by their patient teacher and cured of their ignorance. They came to understand His divine origin. The lesson was now complete. If they were doubting Him before, His followers would follow Him until the ends of the earth now.

†††

This never would have happened had Jesus not forced them onto the boat. This means that as teachers, it is surely great to use free will choosing through differentiation in our instruction in the same way God allows us to choose from right and wrong, but before we do that, it is necessary to unify our students through lessons that are first led by us and second pertinent to all learners so that they will learn to trust us completely.

If we accomplish this task, there will be no limit to what we can accomplish together.

42. Pity for the Fool

Now when Jesus heard this, he withdrew from there in a boat to a lonely place apart. But when the crowds heard it, they followed him on foot from the towns. As he went ashore he saw a great throng; and he had compassion on them, and healed their sick. When it was evening, the disciples came to him and said, "This is a lonely place, and the day is now over; send the crowds away to go into the villages and buy food for themselves." Jesus said, "They need not go away; you give them something to eat."
- Matt. 14:13-16

Mr. T. (born Lawrence Tureaud) is known to many for his role as Clubber Lang in the third instillation of the famous Rocky film series. In his role, he was asked if he "hated" his competitor, Rocky Balboa. He responded with a phrase that would be known for all of time as his calling card, "No. I don't hate Balboa, but I pity the fool."

When taken out of the context of the movie, Mr. T's comment, "I pity the fool" makes perfect Christian sense. Pity, indeed is the feeling that one should feel for people who do not understand Christ's love. But the true test of a Christian is how they respond to that feeling.

Jesus felt pity for the ones who stayed with Him for three days and had nothing to eat. In response to such dejection, He refused to send them away hungry so He did everything in His power to make sure that when they set off on their journeys, they would not collapse in fatigue. 4,000 satisfied people and seven baskets full of extra fragments later, pity was no longer an issue.

†††

As educators, we can relate with both Mr. T and Jesus. Most of our students are full of energy, vibrancy, hope, and curiosity. But then, there are others who simply are not. These are the students who are missing out on the joyful jubilation that the Gospel message has to offer. These are the students who have been searching for truth and have grown weary along the way. How can we not pity them for being less than fully alive? How can we not give them what they need to be satisfied?

Pity without action is highly destructive to any learning environment. To merely feel sorry for a student because of their family situation, their lack of basic skills, or their susceptibility towards misbehavior and to not do anything about it is to send them away hungry and to prolong their suffering until they eventually keel over in exhaustion.

Let us never forget that we, both student and teacher, are one in our journey towards salvation. Without the multiplication of spiritual food that we tie into our lessons, procedures and expectations, we are all bound to collapse along the way.

43. 5 loaves + 2 fish X 1 blessing = A Whole Lot of Holiness

And taking the five loaves and the two fish he looked up to heaven, and blessed, and broke the loaves, and gave them to the disciples to set before the people; and he divided the two fish among them all. And they all ate and were satisfied.
- Mark 6:41-42

The verb "to bless" signifies the sanctification or dedication of a person or thing to some sacred purpose.[28] We see Jesus

---

28 Patrick Morrisroe, "Blessing," The Catholic Encyclopedia. Vol.2. New York: Robert Appleton Company, 1907. 27 Jan. 2015 <http://www.newadvent.org/cathen/02599b.htm>

do this today when He "looked up to Heaven, said the blessing and broke the loaves." In pronouncing this blessing, He took the food that was previously a mere physical source of nutrition and changed it into something holy, or something that has a spiritually pure quality. By doing so, He provided us with an understanding of two things:

1. In this world, there exists an infinite amount of physical things.
2. All of these things can be considered holy if blessed by their creator.

As Christian teachers, we have the ability to recognize that which is holy in many aspects of our vocation: in the fruits of our labor, in the smile of a child, in the warmth of the sun, in the subjects we teach, in the plans that we make, in the execution of our lessons, etc. It is in all things that we recognize the face of God so as to be reminded that we are constantly surrounded by His holy presence.

†††

This recognition is the greatest kindness anyone could possibly share with someone they love. That is why Jesus, after making the five loaves and two fish holy, gives it to those who hunger and thirst. Once fed, "they were satisfied" not so much physically, but spiritually.

This is what we have been sent to do as teachers – to recognize the spiritual aspect of our vocations and to allow Jesus to "bless" our work at every moment. It does us well to come to Him humbly in the deserted place of our hearts and pray with Him, both personally and in community. While in His presence, we should accept His spiritual food and allow it to nourish our souls.

When all this has been carried out, it is then our honor to share this gift with those whom He has called to be our students.

44. Defending Against the Dangers of Academia

And as they went out of Jericho, a great crowd followed him. And behold, two blind men sitting by the roadside, when they heard that Jesus was passing by, cried out, "Have mercy on us, Son of David!" The crowd rebuked them, telling them to be silent; but they cried out the more, "Lord, have mercy on us, Son of David!" And Jesus stopped and called them, saying, "What do you want me to do for you?" They said to him, "Lord, let our eyes be opened." And Jesus in pity touched their eyes, and immediately they received their sight and followed him.
- Matt. 20:29-34

After three attempts to convince His closest followers that He would have to suffer, die and resurrect Himself, Jesus meets two men who believe Him to be God on absolutely no academic basis whatsoever. When He asked them "What do you want me to do for you?" He already knew what they wanted, but to make His point, He wanted these two humble souls to articulate their request in the presence of His closest students so that they too might "have their eyes opened."

Education can be dangerous. To the extent that knowledge can become an addiction, so too does education play a pivotal role in feeding this fire. Too often, people choose to quench the thirst of their intellects instead of their souls. The apostles are a perfect example. They followed Jesus in lock-step for three years and, as a result of listening to his constant lessons, they pieced together only a very shallow understanding of Him. It wasn't until His resurrection that they really and truly figured it out.

†††

In contrast, the blind men, who were surely ostracized from society and uneducated, simply *knew*. How is this possible? Saint Albert the Great tells us how:

"Do you wish to discover the mysteries of God? Ask a man who, for love of God, lives the good news in poverty with joy. He knows the mysteries of God better than the most learned theologian of the earth."[29]

True educators don't let mere academics get in the way of real education. Too often, we are required to teach to a test, bounce from assessment to assessment, crunch data and then decide if our student has "understood" our lessons based on numbers.

Granted, such data can be helpful, but only to a certain extent. True learning spawns those who seek to be taught. While academia can help nurture the motivated student's capacity to comprehend like the disciples, their thirst will never be completely quenched until, like the blind man, their hearts have been opened up by the Master.

45. Failing

In the morning, as he was returning to the city, he was hungry. And seeing a fig tree by the wayside he went to it, and found nothing on it but leaves only. And he said to it, "May no fruit ever come from you again!" And the fig tree withered at once. When the disciples saw it

---

29 *Mscperu.org*, (4 Jan 2015), at http://www.mscperu.org/Santos/santoral/11santos_noviembre.htm, Translated by T.J. Burdick

they marveled, saying, "How did the fig tree wither at once?" And Jesus answered them, "Truly, I say to you, if you have faith and never doubt, you will not only do what has been done to the fig tree, but even if you say to this mountain, 'Be taken up and cast into the sea,' it will be done. And whatever you ask in prayer, you will receive, if you have faith."
- Matt. 21:18-22

It is never a proud moment when a teacher watches his student be led to the waters of knowledge that he so desperately desires to drink of, then fjord through the flowing current in order to arrive at the other side parched, thirsty for what he refuses to consume. It is sad when students "go through the motions" to attain success without truly forcing themselves to acquire new knowledge inwardly, even gloomier when they are so entranced with the habit of school instead of the freedom that education offers them.

When we observe students who are not on fire for their academic success, we desire with our whole hearts that God would light the spark within their souls and lead them along the path that we clear for them. Sometimes, as a result of this intense desire, we hope for their failure.

†††

I know that sounds horrible. After all, teachers are supposed to be a solid rock for their students, always wanting their success, right? Well, to hope that a student fails at being passive, unproductive, and mediocre is the root of the matter. When they have fallen into habits such as these, it is our duty to show them that we as the leader of their learning do not approve. As long as we have done everything within our power to provide for their success, in the event that they still refuse to learn by their own power, it is our duty to fail them. In doing so, we bring their weaknesses to the light and expose them as obstacles holding them back from true success.

Jesus called out the fig tree for its shortcomings. The apostles longed for the ability to do the same. What about us: Are we able to fail our underproductive students to make them better people? Are we ready to be their unwavering rock of council?

46. Being Consistent

Again you have heard that it was said to the men of old, 'You shall not swear falsely, but shall perform to the Lord what you have sworn.' But I say to you, do not swear at all, either by heaven, for it is the throne of God, or by the earth, for it is his footstool, or by Jerusalem, for it is the city of the great King. And do not swear by your head, for you cannot make one hair white or black. Let what you say be simply "Yes" or "No"; anything more than this comes from evil.
- Matt. 5:33-37

Jesus warns us not to chain ourselves to promises because, frankly, we are not worthy enough to make them or strong enough to keep them. Think about it: how can we swear by earthly things if God is their original owner? How can we swear by ourselves if Christ is our inventor? How can we swear by heaven if God has constructed His throne there? We can't, because we are not God. His are the only promises that are true because He is the only Perfect One that can make them.

✝✝✝

As Christian teachers, we find ourselves constantly within the promise of God's will in our lives. When we are able to follow His will consistently and readily during every moment of our day, we become more like Him, thus unifying our efforts to His never-changing source of love.

The best way to do this in our learning environments is by being consistent. When we keep God as the primary source of our teaching, we let our "Yes" mean "Yes," and our "No" mean "No." As a result, our management, delivery, our whole profession becomes part of God. We become His servants who have no need to swear by an oath because we become part of His life-giving promise to the world.

In the grand scheme of things, we are only "dust"[30] and our plans are but "puffs of air."[31] Through our Baptism, however, we became "new creations"[32] who share God's promise of salvation. If we are God's children, why would we need to swear by anything or anyone else?

47. Shock Value

Whoever causes one of these little ones who believe in me to sin, it would be better for him if a great millstone were hung round his neck and he were thrown into the sea. And if your hand causes you to sin, cut it off; it is better for you to enter life maimed than with two hands to go to hell, to the unquenchable fire. And if your foot causes you to sin, cut it off; it is better for you to enter life lame than with two feet to be thrown into hell. And if your eye causes you to sin, pluck it out; it is better for

---

30 Ps. 103:14

31 Ps. 94:11

32 Gal. 6:1

*you to enter the kingdom of God with one eye than with
two eyes to be thrown into hell, where their worm does
not die, and the fire is not quenched.*
- Mark 9:42-48

This Gospel reading is one of the more gruesomely descriptive stories that Jesus ever shared with His disciples. He paints a grotesque picture of what we should do in order to avoid eternal punishment in Hell. These horrid descriptions surely captured the attention of all of His followers because it was so bold and uncharacteristic of Jesus to have stated them. In short, it was shocking!

During the course of our year, our students get used to their daily routines, our teaching styles, and the habitual actions they take part in outside of our learning environment. Like a blur, the same ole' same ole' can become boring and tedious. This situation can be averted if we take a lesson out of Jesus' planning book and fill a few of our sessions with shock value. Like Him, we can paint a picture within our lessons that dives deep into the spiritual core of our students thus requiring a passionate reaction from them. When we pull on their heart strings in this way, they won't just learn, they will actually feel wisdom growing within them.

††††

As a warning, this teaching method can be very dangerous. Such lessons must be delivered with great humility and sensitivity. Before we begin, we must take into account any relevant policy, and concerns our students' parents/guardians might have to these particular lessons. For accountability, run any concerns of these through the respective administrator.

Teaching in an uncharacteristic way like Jesus did challenges our students to open up their eyes to the realities that surround them. When we teach with shock value that requires a wise response, we give them the first sprout of understanding that will eventually lead to full-grown happiness. This is a gift that they will surely accept, but only when their soul has been rocked enough to respond passionately.

48. Doing "Too Much"

You, therefore, must be perfect, as your heavenly Father is perfect.
- Matt. 5:48

The word "perfect" is only mentioned twice in the Gospels. Once when Jesus is referring to the Rich Young Man[33] and the other in today's reading. Since St. Matthew is the author in both instances, we can infer that his inspired message is one of very high expectations. After all, through Him, Jesus tells us that we must be "perfect."

That's raising the bar pretty high don't you think? Reasonably, we are weak, sinful and selfish clumps of dust. We are inclined to sin and imperfection by the constant temptations of the world, and Jesus tells us that we must be "perfect" just like Him? Isn't this asking us to do too much?

Yes, Jesus' request for our perfection is by definition unreasonable, but it is not impossible. As St. Paul wrote in his letter to the Philippians "I can do all things in him who strengthens me."[34] Therefore, perfection is both spiritually and biblically possible if we are able to do "all things" through Christ.

†††

33 Matt. 19:21
34 Phil. 4:13

82

If then, we wish to achieve perfection, we must go beyond our normal efforts and unite our desires to those of the Lord. In other words, we must do more than what is expected of us, we must do "too much." When we commit all of our actions "in Him who strengthens [us]," we discover how to love like Him, how to teach like Him, how to be perfect like Him.

This perfection will resonate in our students like ripples in a pond on a rainy day. When we set the expectations high enough for our students, they too will respond with a supernatural effort to achieve success. When we join their tireless efforts with ours and God's, we prove that perfection is possible for those who are willing to strive too much through Christ.

"Sometimes it is necessary to do too much!"[35]

~Pope John Paul II

49. Teaching with Multiple Intelligences

On the following day, when they came from Bethany, he was hungry. And seeing in the distance a fig tree in leaf, he went to see if he could find anything on it. When he came to it, he found nothing but leaves, for it was not the season for figs. And he said to it, "May no one ever eat fruit from you again." And his disciples heard it.
- Mark 11:12-14

The fig tree was out of season but still had leaves, making it appear as though it would have fruit. It was full of leaves but produced not visible fruit. As a result, Jesus cursed the tree, allowing no one to ever eat of its sweet fruit again. Why? Because it wasn't

---

35 Bill Blakemore, "Beatification of John Paul II: Pope Would Give Candid Interviews – at 35,000 Feet," ABCnews.go.com, (30 Apr 2011), at http://abcnews.go.com/International/beatification-john-paul-ii-pope-give-candid-interviews/story?id=13493166

ready when Jesus needed it.

Sometimes, our students are like the fig tree. They look successful on paper and their grades are fine, but are they really bearing fruit in the classroom or in their community? Are they working as hard as they can? Are they doing so because they are being forced to, perhaps to get a grade and get a nice job in the future? Or are they working hard because they truly want to learn?

Howard Gardener, world-renowned psychologist and Professor of Cognition and Education at Harvard University, conceived a way that we could create fruit among the trees of our students. In his research, he found that all students have a specific way that they are intelligent. In fact, each student has seven ways in which they practice their intelligence; visually, verbally, logically, kinesthetically, interpersonally, intra-personally, and musically.[36] When we find out which one of these multiple intelligences our students are best at using, we will have taken the first step in helping them bear much fruit.

†††

Our next step is to have our students show us that they understand the concepts we are teaching them by using their best intelligence. By producing a drawing (visual), writing a poem (verbal), creating a puzzle (logical), creating a play (kinesthetic), working in groups (interpersonal), working alone (intrapersonal), or singing a song (musical), and many variations of these activities, they can prove to us that they know the material and have fun at the same time.

When we allow our students to show us their understanding of the concepts through their own intelligence, they will begin to put their own personal stamp of originality on their learning and we will begin to see them as they truly are. When these multiple intelligences are practiced, our students will not only be ready for

---

36 *ldpride.net* (4 Jan 2015) at http://www.ldpride.net/learningstyles.MI.htm

the exam, they will be ready to produce true and original fruit among the leaves of success. When we guide them by our Christian example, they will be ready to offer this fruit to Jesus when He comes.

50. Listening to Requests and Giving Surprises

And I tell you, Ask, and it will be given you; seek, and you will find; knock, and it will be opened to you. For every one who asks receives, and he who seeks finds, and to him who knocks it will be opened.
- Luke 11:9-10

During the Christmas season and in the weeks that precede our birthdays, we are sometimes asked to create lists of items that we would like to receive so that others have an idea of the things we want or need. When the day comes for us to receive these gifts, we might be pleased to get these requested items, but there always seems to be at least one person who manages to know us well enough to buy us something that we truly need, but that wasn't on our list. Such unexpected offerings are surprises that might be more useful to our lives in the long run.

Jesus tells the people that if we ask rightly of Him, we will receive. However, He doesn't necessarily say what we will receive. In leaving out exactly what we will get from our petition, He stresses the connection of our will as it pertains to His and not vice versa.

✝✝✝

St. Thomas Aquinas tells us that prayer is "the unfolding of our will to God, that He may fulfill it."[37] Therefore, it is important that we recognize that our prayer requests are merely a plea for confirmation of His will. Since God already knows what we need to complete His will, if we receive what we ask for, we know we are on the same page. However, if we do not receive what we ask for, God has a better gift in mind that He will surprise us with, one that will be more useful to our mission in the long run.

Gifts can only be given in one of two ways – upon request and as a surprise. It would do us well to remember this every time we make a petition to God, every time we listen to our students' requests, and every time we give them the surprise gifts that they truly need.

51. Disciplining for Discipleship

Every one who comes to me and hears my words and does them, I will show you what he is like: he is like a man building a house, who dug deep, and laid the foundation upon rock; and when a flood arose, the stream broke against that house, and could not shake it, because it had been well built. But he who hears and does not do them is like a man who built a house on the ground without a foundation; against which the stream broke, and immediately it fell, and the ruin of that house was great.
- Luke 6:47-49

When we think of the word "discipline," a host of connotations usually come to mind. Negative words like *misbehavior*, *consequences* and *punishment* come to mind and, as a teacher, you know these words become part of your job description. While it is true that there isn't an effective teacher on the planet that really

---

37 *ST III*, q. 21, a. 1

wants to see their pupils suffer, especially at our own hands, it is also true that we will do what is necessary to see them succeed.

Simply put, that means we must discipline them.

†††

Interestingly, the words *disciple* and *discipline* come from the same Latin root word, *discipere*, which means "to grasp intellectually, analyze thoroughly."[38]

In effect, that is exactly what Jesus did throughout His whole ministry; He desired that they would grasp His salvific plan intellectually. His whole management plan was based on commanding the attention in this way. To complete this task, He spoke to small and large audiences, traveled far distances, performed miracles, and even screamed and yelled at times. In everything that He did, He made sure to discipline His disciples in order for them to be ready to grasp the Gospel message intellectually.

You are His modern-day disciple. Therefore, the question remains, are you disciplined enough to receive His truth? Are your students? If not, what do you need to do to ensure that your life is built upon the solid rock of the Master?

52. Using Cause and Effect

Go your way; behold, I send you out as lambs in the midst of wolves. Carry no purse, no bag, no sandals; and salute no one on the road. Whatever house you enter, first say, "Peace be to this house!" And if a son of peace is there, your peace shall rest upon him; but if not, it shall return to you.
- Luke 10:3-6

---

38 Online Etymology Dictionary (4 Jan 2015) at http://www.etymonline.com/index.php?term=disciple

One of Sir Isaac Newton's laws of motion states that "for every action there is an equal and opposite reaction."[39] This law proves true in the physical world every time we throw a tennis ball against a brick wall and it then bounces back to us. As Christian educators, the question we must ask ourselves is whether or not this law is true in the spiritual world as well?

Jesus is in the full swing of His lesson to the apostles in this reading. One of His instructions, however, is quite peculiar. He tells His students "As you enter a house, wish it peace. If the house is worthy, let your peace come upon it; if not, let your peace return to you."

†††

How often do we enter our lessons with high hopes, then become irritated when our students do not understand? How often do we wish all of our students would succeed, but in the end feel responsible for their failures? How often do we wish for peace within our educational psyche, but become all the more frustrated that we have not worked hard enough? These questions spiral inside of our heads whenever we reflect on our teaching. They serve as proof that Newton's laws of physical motion are indeed similar to Jesus' laws of spiritual truth.

All of our actions do indeed have an equal and opposite reaction. Although hopeful, we are frustrated that we can't help everyone. Although giving, we are flustered when our students refuse to accept enlightenment. Although hard-working, we worry that our efforts will not be enough.

Jesus reminds us that our peace must be given to our students. Although we pray that this peace remains inside of them, we must be willing to accept it if it bounces back.

---

39 Sir Isaac Newton, *Mathematical Principles of Natural Philosophy* (1687)

53. Giving Feedback

The apostles returned to Jesus, and told him all that
they had done and taught.
- Mark 6:30

The twelve have returned to the Master after finishing up their mission. We can only imagine how incredibly excited they were to share their experiences, both joyful and painful, with Jesus. Apart from sharing their stories, the apostles surely all came back for one specific reason – they wanted to learn more. They wanted to understand the source of the power they received to do such miraculous things. They probably had gained a dependence on the teachings of their Master to the point that the opinion of others, even their own, meant very little. Ultimately, they wanted feedback.

One of the hardest management skills we struggle with as educators is providing good feedback for our students in response to their work. It takes time to provide a well thought-out comment to share on our students' work and, more often than not, we just don't have enough time to provide it formally. Yet every time they turn in an assignment, raise their hand to ask a question, or merely observe our own actions, they are looking for feedback in the same way Jesus' apostles wanted it.

†††

How can we respond to this "leap of faith" that our students take when they complete their work? We should respond with a few words, formal or informal, written or spoken, to the work they have proudly turned in. When we show them that we have taken their work into consideration on a consistent basis, we give them what they thirst for – approval for a job well done and advice that will help them better their knowledge and understanding.

Although it takes time, so did the work that our students completed. Make sure that the time dedicated to giving feedback to students' work is never less than the amount of time that they deserve for working on it.

54. "Chunking" Information

And one of the scribes came up and heard them disputing with one another, and seeing that he answered them well, asked him, "Which commandment is the first of all?" Jesus answered, "The first is, 'Hear, O Israel: The Lord our God, the Lord is one; and you shall love the Lord your God with all your heart, and with all your soul, and with all your mind, and with all your strength.' The second is this, 'You shall love your neighbor as yourself.' There is no other commandment greater than these."
- Mark 12:28-31

One of the most valuable and oftentimes looked over methods of teaching has its roots in St. Mark's message: "chunking." This means the breaking of large amounts of information into smaller parts so that the learner can remember information better. This method has its advantages when used in moderation, but can be a negative method if overused.

Jesus uses chunking to help His students understand the Mosaic law of the 10 commandments in a better way. To refresh our memory, let's take a look at each commandment as it was written in the time of Moses:

1. You shall have no other God.
2. You shall not misuse the name of the Lord your God.
3. You shall keep Holy the Sabbath.
4. You shall honor your father and your mother.
5. You shall not kill.
6. You shall not commit adultery.
7. You shall not steal.
8. You shall not lie.
9. You shall not want to take your neighbor's wife or husband.
10. You shall not want to take your neighbor's possessions.[40]

†††

When asked which of the 10 commandments is first (or most important), He responds by summarizing all of the Mosaic law into two: "You shall love the Lord your God with all your heart, with all your soul, with all your mind and all your strength... You shall love your neighbor as yourself."[41] By summarizing all into two, Jesus chunked the information and made it easier to follow.

In our learning environments, we too have the ability to chunk the information we teach to make it easier to understand. We must be aware, however, that not all information can be chunked nor should it be. If we overuse chunking, our students might become lazy in their research and, in the process, lose valuable information because they determined that it might have lacked importance. For that reason, we must choose what we chunk sparingly.

---

40 Ex. 20:2-17

41 Mark 12:30-31

Gustav Dore, "Sermon on the Mount," c. 1865
- Wikimedia Commons

55. Understanding God's Report Card

The good man out of his good treasure brings forth good, and the evil man out of his evil treasure brings forth evil. I tell you, on the day of judgment men will render account for every careless word they utter; for by your words you will be justified, and by your words you will be condemned.
– Matt. 12:35-37

Some Christians have a mindset that God is "keeping tabs" on us from above. Like an Olympic judge, some of us believe that He is marking down our every action and grading us on how well we complete our tasks. While this might not be the case, it surely is a logical possibility, especially from the mindset of an educator whose job it is to "keep tabs" on our students both behaviorally and academically.

St. Matthew makes us believe that God surely will judge us by our words and actions. If this is the case, then this is my shot at what His rubric might look like:

	Celestial Intervention Plan	Repentant
Use of Class Time	Constantly worried about self-survival and self-pleasure. Is happy only when satisfied physically. Has little or no time to give to others.	Sees self as a difficult obstacle to conquer. Spends most of his/her time thinking about reasons to believe. Gives (limited) time to those who are close to him/her.
Study Skills	Knows that truth exists, but denies it by his/her lifestyle. Does very little to seek out the truth. Is confused and not orderly.	Accepts truth, but has difficulty understanding it. Often questions the truth but is either too afraid or too lazy to discover answers to these questions. Is somewhat orderly, but often confused.
Ability to Follow Instructions	Hears both sides of conscience often. Responds positively or negatively to the voice within his/her heart. Is progressing slowly or not at all towards understanding the source of this voice.	Reads, comprehends and analyzes the 10 commandments consistently. Can recall the majority of the commandments from memory. Has difficulty accepting consequences when these instructions are not followed to perfection.
Auditory Comprehension	Feels attracted by an unknown, invisible force within nature, but responds negatively towards it. Denies existence of a voice greater than his/hers. Has difficulty listening to others.	Hears the voice of reason clearly and responds to it within the confines of a scheduled time. Frequently makes requests to God, but rarely thanks Him for graces already received. Is able to listen to others successfully, but would rather do most of the talking.
Reading Comprehension	Reads rules written on his/her heart. Either reflects on these laws often or never. Rarely or never reads spiritual texts.	Reads spiritual texts to gain information necessary for personal salvation. Accepts each word as truth and rarely channels or challenges their true source.
Participation	Prefers to work individually. Rarely visits a house of worship. Participates primarily in activities suited to his/her sensorial pleasure.	Is able to work with others, but rarely volunteers to share knowledge. Goes to Church every once in a while. Doubts whether or not he/she is able to give up personal pleasures for charitable actions.
Behavior	Jesus-less	Jesus-seeking

On Fire	Saintly
Takes risks in charitable actions. Steps outside his/her own comfort zone. Enjoys trying new things, even when outcomes are unsuccessful. Is developing a craving for serving others.	Recognizes God in every action committed by him/her or others. Is satisfied only by the spiritual undertones of charity. Has dedicated his/her life to the perpetual success of God's Kingdom.
Accepts the truth and frequently seeks out trustworthy sources to back up his/her research. Often delighted by the answers he/she discovers, but questions still remain. Rarely shows confusion.	Accepts the truth and lives it habitually. Allows the truth to work within him/her instead of relying on personal inspirations. Still questions truths often, but immediately seeks heavenly counsel. Is joyful by nature, so much so that others yearn to be as happy as him/her.
Chunks the 10 commandments into 2 that are smaller & easier to remember*. Recalls them frequently throughout the week, but mostly limits their usage to Church. Frequently accepts grace or struggle as part of their spiritual growth. *Mark 12: 28-31	Chunks original 10 commandments into 1 that is smaller and easier to remember*. Allows Christ to work from within in all areas not just at Church. Always accepts both grace and struggle as part of God's plan. *John 13: 34
Sets aside a little extra time to speak with God. Has some difficulty calming his/herself to enter into His presence. Makes requests, but also thanks Him for answered prayers and other blessings. Can listen fairly well to His voice, but gets distracted from time to time.	Has found truth in silence. Speaks only when necessary both to God and to others. Is humbled by His inaudible messages within nature, daily activities, others, and self. Takes every moment possible to place him/herself in His presence so as to rely on, thank, and adore Him.
Reads spiritual texts to gain proof for personal growth or to defend personal beliefs against others. Is progressing towards understanding their true source. Asks questions about what he/she reads.	Reads all texts through the lens of spirituality in order to provide his/her soul with holy sustenance. Has built a relationship with their true source and imitated His example as "The Word Made Flesh." Is able to give confident answers to those who ask questions.
Works fairly well with others. Volunteers often to share knowledge and experience with peers. Has given up some personal pleasures and replaced them with charitable actions.	Lives for others. Provides peers with a quasi-mystical example of faith and morale. Frequently found in Church beyond required celebration days. Always available to help in any way.
Jesus-like	It is no longer he/she who lives, but Christ within him/her* *Galatians 2:20

"Rendering an account" for Jesus will surely take place after we die, but it can also happen during our lifetimes. It would be in our best interest to examine our conscience often (perhaps even using the rubric above) so as to refer to the portfolio of our souls and ensure that our work is polished, immaculate, and His.

56. Deciphering Intentions

Then some of the scribes and Pharisees said to him, "Teacher, we wish to see a sign from you." But he answered them, "An evil and adulterous generation seeks for a sign; but no sign shall be given to it except the sign of the prophet Jonah."
- Matt. 12:38-39

Students have a way of setting the pace for instruction. Their behavior, questions, and work habits tend to guide the way we teach more often than our own inhibitions at times. More often than not, students do not realize this power, but every once in a while, a rather intelligent student or two drifts away from the current and attempts to lead the rest into rough waters.

The scribes and Pharisees cleverly attempted to pull the balance of power to their side in a similar way in this lesson's reading. They tried to mask their malicious intentions by acting like they were truly interested in Christ's teachings. They called him "Teacher," then asked Him to teach by requesting a "sign." Little did they know that this sign was Jesus Himself. Had their intentions been true, they would have no need to make such a request; they would have already believed.

†††

For the most part, our students are genuinely interested in making sense of what they learn from us. When they ask questions, make comments, and request clarity, they truly mean well. However, like the Pharisees, some have a hidden, more distracting agenda in mind. Being able to know when a student's intentions are pure and when they are not is one of the qualities of a great teacher.

Jesus knew when His students were well versus ill-intentioned because He could see into their hearts. We, on the other hand, are only able to receive glimpses of their motives. May we consult with Jesus in our times of doubt so that we can see their souls as He does and guide them to the high expectation of purity in their actions. Perhaps then, they will recognize within us the "sign" that they seek.

57. Journeying Into the Unknown

He said therefore, "What is the kingdom of God like? And to what shall I compare it? It is like a grain of mustard seed which a man took and sowed in his garden; and it grew and became a tree, and the birds of the air made nests in its branches."
- Luke 13:18-19

According to a National Geographic Daily News article published online in the summer of 2011, it is estimated that 86% of Earth's animal species are still unknown.[42] If we multiply that by

---

42 Traci Watson, "86 Percent of Earth's Species Still Unknown?" *National Geographic News* (24 Aug 2011) at http://news.nationalgeographic.com/news/2011/08/110824-earths-species-8-7-million-biology-planet-animals-science/

the amount of unknown knowledge within the realms of biology, mathematics, physics, astronomy, theology, etc. we come to the sobering conclusion that we don't know everything. In fact, when it comes to pure, unaltered and scientifically proven facts, we know very little.

For Christians, this idea isn't new. We know that God is the creator of all things and we recognize ourselves as "specks of dust"[43] in His presence. We know that "the foolishness of God is wiser than men, and the weakness of God is stronger than men."[44] The unknown for us, therefore, is kind of exhilarating because we constantly ponder it in our hearts as He reveals it to us through grace every day.

†††

God's knowledge is perfect. Our knowledge, with the nurturing of Christ, has the ability to grow so great that we graze the heavens with our boughs where our students, as birds, may rest comfortably.

As educators, we have been blessed with a multitude of wavelengths to understand both the known and the unknown. It is our job to be as informed as possible about the subjects we teach and to challenge our students to follow our lead into the unknown. The journey toward discovery, imagination, and invention is where we find God, Who then gives us the answers we seek.

58. Getting Away

And they rose up and put him out of the city, and led him to the brow of the hill on which their city was built, that they might throw him down headlong. But passing

---

43 Job 30:19
44 1 Cor. 1:25

through the midst of them he went away.
- Luke 4:29-30

There comes a moment for every educator when they can no longer bear the burdens of teaching. The discomfort we sense from being inside the classroom and the overbearing amounts of work to be done tend to weigh heavy on us.

In this reading, Jesus may have felt a similar burden. After reading the scroll and admitting that He was, indeed the Savior that the prophet Isaiah was speaking of, the people of His hometown became infuriated and wanted to toss Him off of a cliff. What did He do in response? He finished His parables and went away so that His students could benefit from His absence. Simple as that.

†††

When the burdens of teaching are laid across our back, we know that they have been placed there by Christ Himself so that we can share in His passion for the redemption of souls. While we suffer, it is important that we first finish what needs to be done, like Jesus finished His parables. Once our work is done and our spirits exhausted from the struggle, we can then offer our struggles to God who will joyfully take our crosses upon His back so that we can rest for a while.

Those days when you find yourself burdened or weighed down, find a moment to get away with God. Not only will you need the rest, but your students will benefit from your refreshment as well.

59. Using Discretion

Then Pharisees and scribes came to Jesus from Jerusalem and said, "Why do your disciples transgress

the tradition of the elders? For they do not wash their hands when they eat." He answered them, "And why do you transgress the commandment of God for the sake of your tradition? For God commanded, 'Honor your father and your mother,' and, 'He who speaks evil of father or mother, let him surely die.' But you say, 'If any one tells his father or his mother, What you would have gained from me is given to God, he need not honor his father.' So, for the sake of your tradition, you have made void the word of God. You hypocrites! Well did Isaiah prophesy of you, when he said: 'This people honors me with their lips, but their heart is far from me; in vain do they worship me, teaching as doctrines the precepts of men.'"
– Matt. 15:1-9

Like the elders in the reading, our own learning environments resound with antique traditions that work to prevent teachers from providing students with true learning. In an effort to "universalize" education, the world has sought to create the same expectations for every student of every culture in every region. When multiplied by the data measurement abilities that technology provides, a unique threat to teacher discretion becomes painfully present: reliance on fallible data.

Granted, the philosophy behind standardized testing can be rendered coherent. Surely we cannot eliminate order or formal assessment all together. Statistical facts can provide quality and effective data-driven instruction. However, we must recognize the reality that too much stress on numbers in education compromises teacher discretion, which is the crux of effective teaching.

††††

Jesus knew that the elders had become so wrapped up in their traditions that they had forgotten how to think logically and spiritually. The daily routine had taken over their entire culture, and recognizing the needs of His people, He geared His instruction towards the discovery of truth behind the walls of tradition that blocked them from it.

Since Christ, humans have benefitted from their giant intellects and creativity in light of His gifts of wisdom and understanding. When it is necessary, it would be in our best interest to imitate His actions and use our discretion to evaluate the way things are done in our curriculums as a whole. When we answer these questions honestly, we will come to the realization that He is, in fact, the only thing that is truly "universal" in us.

60. Weathering the Storms

He also said to the multitudes, "When you see a cloud rising in the west, you say at once, 'A shower is coming'; and so it happens. And when you see the south wind blowing, you say, 'There will be scorching heat'; and it happens. You hypocrites! You know how to interpret the appearance of earth and sky; but why do you not know how to interpret the present time?"
- Luke 12:54-56

Weather has a tremendous effect on our behaviors. According to recent psychological studies, heat and extreme rain bring about the worst in people and, on the other hand, higher temperatures can bring a depressed person up.[45] Consequently, mood phe-

---

45 John M. Grohol, Psy, D. "Can Weather Affect Your Mood?" *psychcentral. com* (29 Aug 2014) at http://psychcentral.com/blog/archives/2014/08/29/can-weather-affect-your-mood/

nomena that include Seasonal Affective Disorder and Full Moon Insomnia[46] also play a part in our daily routines that can have a devastating effect on the learning process.

Jesus speaks of the correlation between the physical weather of the world and the spiritual storm that was building up everywhere He set His holy feet. He explained that they were not able to live their lives according to the rhythm of the truths that He was instructing them and yet, they were perfectly apt in recognizing the routine effects that weather had upon them and their lives.

†††

Jesus acknowledges that the weather is something we can predict. Modern psychology has proven that weather patterns are also able to affect our behaviors. However, according to the Master, it is more important that we are able to recognize first the celestial truths that dwell in the hearts of all men and women, so that we can properly predict, prepare for and survive the spiritual storms that rage within our souls.

As we prepare for our day today, and if the weather allows, perhaps a bit of the outdoors would do well for both our students and for our minds, bodies, and souls. As you gaze skyward, allow the signs of the current weather pattern to infiltrate itself into your own personal examination of conscience. Only when you examine yourself interiorly will you be able to examine similar spiritual patters in the souls of your students.

Then and only then will you truly be able to weather any storm.

---

46 Steve Morales, "Full Moon Causes Poorer Sleep Study Finds", *CBC News* (25 Jul 2013) at http://www.cbc.ca/news/health/full-moon-causes-poorer-sleep-study-finds-1.1322612

61. Grouping Students

Now about eight days after these sayings he took with him Peter and John and James, and went up on the mountain to pray. And as he was praying, the appearance of his countenance was altered, and his raiment became dazzling white. And behold, two men talked with him, Moses and Elijah, who appeared in glory and spoke of his departure, which he was to accomplish at Jerusalem. Now Peter and those who were with him were heavy with sleep, and when they wakened they saw his glory and the two men who stood with him. And as the men were parting from him, Peter said to Jesus, "Master, it is well that we are here; let us make three booths, one for you and one for Moses and one for Elijah" – not knowing what he said. As he said this, a cloud came and overshadowed them; and they were afraid as they entered the cloud. And a voice came out of the cloud, saying, "This is my Son, my Chosen; * listen to him!" And when the voice had spoken, Jesus was found alone. And they kept silence and told no one in those days anything of what they had seen.
- Luke 9:28-36

Peter, James and John were able to be with Jesus and experience Him and His glory in more ways than the other Apostles. They were the only three present during the transfiguration in this reading. They were the only three allowed to enter the house of Jairus to witness the resurrection of his daughter.[47] They were the only three that accompanied Jesus during the agony of the garden.[48] In fact, John, commonly referred to as "the disciple that Je-

---

47 Mark 5:37
48 Mark 14:33

sus loved," was the only apostle to be present at the crucifixion.[49]

Why, then, were these three given the opportunity to have this "extra time" with Jesus? Here are three reasons that Jesus might have called this particular "small group" of students together:

1. They, like some of our overachievers, were restless and begged Jesus to take them everywhere. They searched above and beyond for moments to be close to Jesus so that they could understand Him and his teachings. They were quite possibly Jesus' "teacher's pets."

2. They were "advanced" learners like those little geniuses that we have such difficulty challenging in our classrooms. Jesus, the best teacher in the history of the world, wanted them to follow Him closer so that they could achieve higher standards of His truth.

3. They were "underachievers" that needed the extra help to understand the truth better while the other Apostles already understood and didn't need as much "hands-on" experience.

So which group would explain these three Apostles best? All three.

Biblically, John, "the disciple that Jesus loved," is constantly portrayed as youthful, restless, and much like a teacher's pet.

James is commonly understood to be the most thorough when it came to the Christian law (read his letter in the New Testament as well as Acts of the Apostles for examples), thus making him an advanced learner.

Lastly, Peter finds himself putting his foot in his mouth more often than not which would make him more of an underachiever.

†††

---

49 John 19:26

Jesus was able to lead this "small group" and other "large groups" successfully because He was able to identify each individual's strengths and weaknesses. Although John was a teacher's pet, he was restless. Although James was advanced, he was determined. Although Peter was ignorant at times, he was still a great leader. These strengths made up for their weaknesses. In the end, these worldly fishermen of old became professionals in moral virtue and pioneers of selfless charity. Together, they built the Church and gained what they were incapable of attaining individually – eternal life.

Like the Apostles, our learning environments are filled with different personalities and talents. The next time we form learning groups, we, like the Master, must be able to identify the strengths and weaknesses of our students and pair them evenly so that they will succeed in the tasks we assign to them. If we really want to go the extra mile and imitate Christ, our students will be able to work together to achieve something more important than mere grades – they might achieve the transformation of their souls and consequently, eternal life.

62. Seamless Teaching

And as they were coming down the mountain, Jesus commanded them, "Tell no one the vision, until the Son of man is raised from the dead." And the disciples asked him, "Then why do the scribes say that first Elijah must come?" He replied, "Elijah does come, and he is to restore all things; but I tell you that Elijah has already come, and they did not know him, but did to him whatever they pleased. So also the Son of man will suffer at their hands." Then the disciples understood that he was speaking to them of John the Baptist.
- Matt. 17:9-13

Words and actions have a way of working together to help people understand concepts. Think about the Mass, we have the Liturgy of the Word as combined with the Liturgy of the Eucharist. During the Liturgy of the Word, we listen to the written word of God through scripture. When we celebrate the Eucharist, we witness the sacrificial act of the Last Supper and take part in the eating of His body and the drinking of His blood. The entire service is balanced by both word and act in a seamless rhythm of celestial importance.

Jesus highlighted an interwoven story of His own in this reading: He first journeyed back to the Old Testament prophecy regarding Elijah then seconded with another about John the Baptist. Finally, He connected the two with His own self and *voila!* His disciples understood what He was talking about!

†††

The sharing of personal stories is a must in teaching. It turns us into human beings as opposed to lecturing fact fanatics and giver-outers of homework. It also allows us to grow in relationship with our students and the subjects we relate our stories to as well.

However, there is also a presupposition that if you are able to share any story at all, that you must have first lived through the occurrence in order to speak about it with credibility. In actuality, the act is transmitted into words and consequently, meaning can turn into understanding on the students' part if given the proper context within your lesson delivery. This balance between word and act is exactly what Jesus did and it is exactly what we should imitate.

An effective teacher is only as good as his or her stories. When we can seamlessly weave our lives into our work there is a good possibility that our students will become a part of it. When we let God do the spooling, our seams will never burst.

63. Having a Sense of Humor

When they came to Capernaum, the collectors of the half-shekel tax went up to Peter and said, "Does not your teacher pay the tax?" He said, "Yes." And when he came home, Jesus spoke to him first, saying, "What do you think, Simon? From whom do kings of the earth take toll or tribute? From their sons or from others?" And when he said, "From others," Jesus said to him, "Then the sons are free. However, not to give offense to them, go to the sea and cast a hook, and take the first fish that comes up, and when you open its mouth you will find a shekel; take that and give it to them for me and for yourself."
- Matt. 17:24-27

Teachers have an arsenal of funny stories that involve our colleagues, learning environments, experiences and, above all others, our students. There are very few educators in the world who are unable to think back to a moment of intense laughter that was sparked by something a student said or did.

This works both ways. Just about every student can recall a time when their teachers made them chuckle, giggle or even cry with laughter at something hilarious that they said or did.

After being questioned about the temple tax, Peter was given a most humorous task to complete: he had to get the coins to pay for Jesus and himself in quite a peculiar way. We can be sure that this particular miracle must have put a smile on the husky fisherman's face.

†††

Surely, Peter never forgot this experience. Had Jesus merely made the coin appear out of thin air like a magician or, even worse if He had made Peter work selling fish like he did every day of his life prior to meeting Jesus, then there is no way he would have remembered it.

Teaching is a very entertaining profession, but let us not be the only ones being entertained by the natural hilarity that our students come by in the cleverness or innocence of their youth. Rather, let's slip a little humor into our lessons so that they too can benefit from one of the most effective teaching traits that every son or daughter of God has – our senses of humor.

Go ahead, you can be lighthearted. Jesus was (and still is).

64. Creating Peer Relationships

And when Jesus heard it, he said to him, "One thing you still lack. Sell all that you have and distribute to the poor, and you will have treasure in heaven; and come, follow me." But when he heard this he became sad, for he was very rich. Jesus looking at him said, "How hard it is for those who have riches to enter the kingdom of God! For it is easier for a camel to go through the eye of a needle than for a rich man to enter the kingdom of God." Those who heard it said, "Then who can be saved?" But he said, "What is impossible with men is possible with God." And Peter said, "Lo, we have left our homes and followed you." And he said to them, "Truly, I say to you, there is no man who has left house or wife or brothers or parents or children, for the sake of the kingdom of God, who will not receive manifold more in this time, and in the age to come eternal life."
- Luke 18:22-30

To be able to identify what students need most, but want the least, is a tremendous talent. Teaching this, however, is almost impossible. Why? Because in order for the student to learn, they must will it and as all teachers know, this isn't always the case.

Jesus had a similar conundrum when He attempted to teach the young rich man what he needed to achieve spiritual perfection. The lesson turned sour as the young rich man was saddened by the Master's words.

In an instant, Peter spoke up almost gloating in the rich young man's face about how he and the other disciples had "given everything" in order to follow the Master. What happened to the young rich man, we do not know, but would this story have been different had Peter extended his hand in friendship to welcome the rich young man into discipleship as opposed to bragging about his sacrifice?

†††

Most of our students have an aversion to school much like the young rich man had to Christ's words. Mandatory education isn't a huge motivator for them and as a result, teachers struggle to find ways to light a spark within the souls of their students.

While learning for the sake of learning isn't always the highest of our students' priorities, friendships and social perception are. When we use our students' relationships in our instruction, we build on their foundation of trust. If we can use each student's personality to build on the foundation we have set in our lessons by focusing on the key relationships they have with each other so as to build an effective working environment, they will not only achieve individually, but their friends will benefit as well.

65. Being Accountable

And when he entered the temple, the chief priests and the elders of the people came up to him as he was teaching, and said, "By what authority are you doing these things, and who gave you this authority?" Jesus answered them, "I also will ask you a question; and if you tell me the answer, then I also will tell you by what authority I do these things. The baptism of John, whence was it? From heaven or from men?" And they argued with one another, "If we say, 'From heaven,' he will say to us, 'Why then did you not believe him?' But if we say, 'From men,' we are afraid of the multitude; for all hold that John was a prophet." So they answered Jesus, "We do not know." And he said to them, "Neither will I tell you by what authority I do these things."
- Matt. 21:23-27

At the end of every school year, one of the things I do is meet up with a colleague of mine to talk about how well or how poorly our year went. We typically wait until we have had enough time to rest and reflect so that when we do meet, we can call each other out on our imperfections and celebrate our triumphs. It is a time we both look forward to and dread because we subject ourselves to holding nothing back.

Today's world sees talks like these as threatening and politically incorrect. They fear accountability because it challenges their consciences and infringes upon their freedom. The "I don't need anybody" and "I can do this myself" attitude springs forth in contemporary culture and a series of unfortunate events ensues.

Jesus addresses the importance of accountability in all of our actions. He could very easily revealed to whom He was accountable to those seeking to find from whom His authority came, but instead, He chose to test them. He pitted their personal beliefs against their image. In cornering them in this way, Jesus made them choose to whom they would be accountable – to themselves or to God. They chose the former and were left empty-handed because of their lack of trust in the Master.

†††

Accountability requires people to humble themselves. A certain degree of trust must be established in such a relationship. Trust and humility are two aspects of life that most would prefer to do without, but they are the foundations of all progress.

Jesus never allows His disciples to discern His teachings alone. Let us be humbled by the critiques of our peers, joyful for their guidance, and zealous to teach our children how to be accountable to one another just as we are to our colleagues and to God.

66. Staying Healthy

What do you think? A man had two sons; and he went to the first and said, "Son, go and work in the vineyard today." And he answered, "I will not"; but afterward he repented and went. And he went to the second and said the same; and he answered, "I go, sir," but did not go. Which of the two did the will of his father? They said, "The first." Jesus said to them, "Truly, I say to you, the tax collectors and the harlots go into the kingdom of God before you. For John came to you in the way of righteousness, and you did not believe him, but the tax collectors and the harlots believed him; and even when you saw it, you did not afterward repent and

believe him."
- Matt. 21:28-32

Children go through what some call the "terrible twos." During this time, to most of the requests we make, like a reflex, children protest. This displays an innate truth that humans seem to be born with: an inclination to do what we shouldn't.

We are like the two-year-old children of God. We are surrounded by a multitude of temptations and vices and our free will tends to want to delve into them completely at whatever cost. We are susceptible to sin and enticed by the temporary pleasures that it can provide us.

St. Paul reminds us of our spiritual immaturity when he wrote, "Brothers, I could not talk to you as spiritual people, but as fleshly people, as infants in Christ. I fed you milk, not solid food, because you were unable to take it. Indeed, you are still not able, even now."[50]

†††

This reading shows the mark of a true disciple of Christ: that he or she does God's will even when he or she doesn't feel like doing it. That first call is the most difficult because we know that if we answer it, we must deny our sinful appetites and begin to drink the spiritual milk that St. Paul spoke of in his letter to the Corinthians.

Teachers have the task of serving up an academic meal rich with the nutrition of truth and virtue. Before we can do that, however, we must first be Christ's true disciple and have a healthy diet of all of the celestial nutrition that the Master provides us with through prayer, contemplation, study and work. Only when we achieve spiritual maturity will we be able to become Master Chefs

---

50 1 Cor. 3:2

that can serve up a piping hot lesson filled with the ingredients of faith, hope and love.

67. Overgeneralizing

And behold, a lawyer stood up to put him to the test, saying, "Teacher, what shall I do to inherit eternal life?" He said to him, "What is written in the law? How do you read?" And he answered, "You shall love the Lord your God with all your heart, and with all your soul, and with all your strength, and with all your mind; and your neighbor as yourself." And he said to him, "You have answered right; do this, and you will live."
- Luke 10:25-28

Jesus had a masterful way of simplifying His instruction. In response to the man's inquiry on how to inherit eternal life from this reading, Jesus responded by testing the man's knowledge of "the law." The complete Jewish law was composed of 613 commandments that are found in the book of Leviticus.[51] You can imagine, then, that when posed with Christ's response, "What is written in the law?" the lawyer might have been shaking in his sandals at the possible expectation of the Master's request.

His response, however, was educational gold: an overgeneralization.

Overgeneralizing our instruction means to take the whole of the lesson in all of its complexity and to speak of it in general terms in order for our students to grasp the fundamental principles of the meaning we wish for them to retain.

---

51 Tracy R. Rich, "A List of the Mitzvot" at *jewfaq.org* (4 Jan 2014) at http://www.jewfaw.org/613

†††

Here's an example. If one wants their students to write using correct punctuation (and actually enjoy the writing process), he might give them a general topic to write about prior to teaching them the skill of using punctuation. Once they are finished writing, he can teach them the skill and revise their work with them to correct their punctuation errors. By overgeneralizing the first portion of his instruction, his students write a personal narrative (and hopefully enjoy writing it) and in the end, they learn how to punctuate correctly.

If, however, he teaches the punctuation skill first, odds are their writing will be forced, restricted to the grammar rule learned as opposed to free and joyful exuberance that writing should exude.

The lawyer in this reading overgeneralized. Jesus overgeneralized. Such methodology forces our intellects to rely on our analytical minds to first accept them as true then revise what we believe to be true with countless corrections.

Our teaching should have the same effect.

68. Becoming the Student

But he said to them, "How can they say that the Christ is David's son? For David himself says in the Book of Psalms, 'The Lord said to my Lord, Sit at my right hand, till I make thy enemies a stool for thy feet.' David thus calls him Lord; so how is he his son?"
- Luke 20:41-44

In the 2008 comedy *Tenure*, a young college professor attempts to jump through the hoops of a small university in hopes to ensure a position on the collegiate level for life. After many failed attempts to achieve tenure status, the main character receives applause from his boss for all of the feedback he had received from the students who took his courses. When asked how he was able to connect with them so well, the main character responded, "I try never to forget what it felt like to be a student."

Many times we, the teachers, find ourselves in a juxtaposition in which the students are able to teach us a thing or two. Sometimes, we are too proud to admit it while other times we are open to their knowledge. In either case, the fact that the student can become the teacher should be a complement to our work.

††††

Jesus refers to Himself as the Messiah that David referred to as "Lord," but David was a mere mortal. As a servant, Jesus humbled Himself in assuming a human nature in union with His divine nature, and as a result, He was able to be used as an instrument of obedience.

Teachers must achieve this ability to lower ourselves as real servants. Through Jesus, we are destined for greatness, but until we are able to place ourselves below our students, our intellectual and spiritual talents will mean nothing and both student and teacher will cease to grow. Granted, we are given the responsibility to care and nurture them to the best of our ability, but when it comes time for us to step down from our high horse, we must be humble enough to teach our students how to handle the reigns.

69. Meaningless Work

And the Pharisees and the scribes asked him, "Why do your disciples not live according to the tradition of the elders, but eat with hands defiled?" And he said to

*them, "Well did Isaiah prophesy of you hypocrites, as
it is written, 'This people honors me with their lips, but
their heart is far from me; in vain do they worship me,
teaching as doctrines the precepts of men.' You leave
the commandment of God, and hold fast the tradition
of men."*
- Mark 7:5-8

This reading from Mark's Gospel refers to the Jewish tradition of washing one's hands before eating. This tradition was established to draw closer to God in purity. Over time, however, the Pharisees and Scribes had deformed this belief into something much less than its original intention. The once "holy" tradition had turned into a senseless method of superstition.

We are presented with the same temptation of following "senseless traditions." We find ourselves making empty promises, overlooking negative behavior, and practicing meaningless teaching pedagogies that we know are not effective. We even find ways to waste time on our computers or in the hallways between classes. We follow these traditions habitually because that is "how we have always done things." Such traditions can be dangerous to our educational health if we don't do something to change them.

††††

This reading encourages us to return to what should be the source of our actions, namely God's will. With a little creativity and a lot of hard work, our senseless traditions can easily be changed into "holy" actions that actually benefit the education of our students. By calling to mind the presence of God in our work, we refocus our sight on the will of God and away from our meaningless traditions. When we can habitually combine His will with our own, we understand what Saint Paul meant when he commanded us to "pray constantly."[52]

For this reason, the disciples didn't need to wash their hands before eating; for they were already purified by the presence of Jesus.

May our classrooms be a part of that same presence.

70. Building Confidence

For they all saw him, and were terrified. But immediately he spoke to them and said, "Take heart, it is I; have no fear." And he got into the boat with them and the wind ceased. And they were utterly astounded, for they did not understand about the loaves, but their hearts were hardened.
- Mark 6:50-52

Jesus knew that the spiritual task He was proposing to His disciples during the storm was difficult, if not impossible. He wanted them to construct a faith inside themselves based on the Gospel truth that they did not completely understand. By allowing them to suffer and watching them as they progressed against the storm, He knew that they would eventually lose their faith to their need for survival.

He knew it, but never acted upon it…until now.

We send our students into the unknown to work alone in the same way Jesus sent His disciples to sea. There, they are sure to struggle enough to begin losing their faith in themselves or in others. When this happens, it is up to us to come close enough that they realize that we are not "ghosts" waiting for their eventual death, but saviors coming to help them. As we come into focus, we too must seemingly "walk on water" in order to enter the boat, to calm the storm, and to help them get to a place they cannot reach by themselves.

---

52 1 Thes. 5:17

†††

When all of their efforts have failed is when we, like Jesus, must give in and offer our services. If we learn to recognize when our students are struggling, we don't become their crutch, but we do become their shepherd. Some ways to do this would include hinting at correct answers, helping our students think critically, or guiding them toward a source where they can find the answers to their questions. By giving them the tools necessary to overcome their obstacles, we calm their seas and motivate them to do more.

In the words of English missionary James Hudson Taylor, "There are three stages in the work of God; impossible, difficult, done." One cannot go from "impossible" to "done"[53] without a teacher to help them through the "difficult." May we be this teacher for our students and may Jesus be this teacher for us all.

71. Interruptions

While he was still speaking, there came from the ruler's house some who said, "Your daughter is dead. Why trouble the Teacher any further?" But ignoring what they said, Jesus said to the ruler of the synagogue, "Do not fear, only believe."
- Mark 5:35-36

This reading starts with an interruption: "While Jesus was still speaking, people from the synagogue official's house arrived and said, 'your daughter has died.'"

Someone interrupted the woman who had already interrupted Jesus. Remember, Jesus would not even have been speaking

---

53 Lyall, Leslie T., *A Passion for the Impossible: The Continuing Story of the Mission Hudson Taylor Began.* (London: OMF Books, 1965)

had it not been for the woman who touched His clothes and interrupted His travels. In point of fact, Jesus was originally interrupted by Jairus when He arrived on shore from Gerasenes where He more than likely was going to tell another parable about the Kingdom for the people of that area. Even still, at Gerasenes, He was interrupted by the poor man with a legion of demons. Even before *that,* Jesus' sleep was interrupted by His worried disciples and a rather vicious storm that needed some calming.

Jesus' life was filled with interruptions that He gladly welcomed. Being an all knowing and all powerful God who chose to live as a human, we can assume that these "interruptions" weren't interruptions at all. Rather, they were the places where God intended His Son to be for the sake of His will. They were tasks given to Jesus to complete that weren't necessarily planned, but very much welcomed.

†††

As teachers, we must also be ready for the unexpected. Some have heard the phrase, "If you want to make God laugh, make plans." Being educators, we can find the humor in that statement because we know that some things just don't go according to plan. When that time comes, it is our job to recognize it as out of our control and, "not be afraid," as Jesus tells us.

Being busy, we must be intent on unifying our plans with those of our supreme guide: Jesus. When we focus our efforts on His love, we find that our plans become His. Then, it is truly Him that moves us to the places we need to be, the conversations we need to be a part of, and the positions we fill to carry out His will.

As former Congressionalist Minister of Scotland George MacDonald put it, "I find that doing the will of God leaves me no time for disputing about His plans."[54]

---

54 *Goodreads.com* (4 Jan. 2015) at http://www.goodreads.com/author/quotes/2413.George_MacDonald

His Passion and Our Mission

I am sure you have discovered by now that teaching isn't as easy as many believe it to be. It is, in fact, the hardest job that anyone can do, being a homeschooler or a university professor. In fact, St. James even tells us, "Let not many of you become teachers."[55] Thanks, St. James. That is information that would have been great to know before we began teaching!

Truth be told, there is nothing worth earning that doesn't require struggle. Christ demonstrated this on Calvary and you demonstrate it every time you show up for work. Like St. Paul, you make up for what is lacking in Christ's suffering.[56]

Be strong. There's victory for all who persevere to the end.[57]

72. Knowing It All

Six days before the Passover, Jesus came to Bethany, where Lazarus was, whom Jesus had raised from the dead. There they made him a supper; Martha served,

---

55 James 3:1
56 Col. 1:24
57 James 1:12

and Lazarus was one of those at table with him. Mary took a pound of costly ointment of pure nard and anointed the feet of Jesus and wiped his feet with her hair; and the house was filled with the fragrance of the ointment. But Judas Iscariot, one of his disciples (he who was to betray him), said, "Why was this ointment not sold for three hundred denarii and given to the poor?" This he said, not that he cared for the poor but because he was a thief, and as he had the money box he used to take what was put into it. Jesus said, "Let her alone, let her keep it for the day of my burial."
- John 12:1-7

Some students enjoy thinking they know everything. True? They interrupt lessons, are sometimes defiant and they might even undermine our authority. They showcase their "abilities" often, but why? Shouldn't the student be the most responsive to our teachings? Aren't they the ones that come to *us* to learn?

The answer to this question is in us. You know those adults who think they know everything? Well, they affect their environment in much the same way that a know-it-all student would. What's worse is that our students take notice and imitate them. In the end, stubborn role models who are unable to humble themselves pass their ignorance down to children who, like the mirrors they are, reflect their elders.

†††

The apostles had the same habits that they learned from the Jewish officials that raised them. Only Jesus could see through them and called them out on the true meaning behind Mary's actions in the reading. The beauty of her kind act would have been lost had it been taken as the waste that the "know-it-all" apostles claimed it to be.

Your learning environment is filled with know-it-alls who need you to help them know it all. The only person who can teach them the beauty and truth behind what we teach is Jesus. And with Him, you can learn it all.

73. Following Multi-Step Directions

And on the first day of Unleavened Bread, when they sacrificed the passover lamb, his disciples said to him, "Where will you have us go and prepare for you to eat the passover?" And he sent two of his disciples, and said to them, "Go into the city, and a man carrying a jar of water will meet you; follow him, and wherever he enters, say to the householder, 'The Teacher says, Where is my guest room, where I am to eat the passover with my disciples?' And he will show you a large upper room furnished and ready; there prepare for us." And the disciples set out and went to the city, and found it as he had told them; and they prepared the passover.
- Mark 14:12-16

One of our daily activities is to get our students from point "A" to point "B." As we all know, however, it isn't always so simple. When confusion and uncertainty sets in, our quest for raising our students' understanding of concepts becomes a bit more difficult. As a result, the process to get from point "A" to point "B" sub-categorizes into many smaller steps. This is when we begin giving multi-step directions.

Jesus gives two of His disciples the task of starting from outside of the city (point "A") to going into the city and preparing for the Passover meal (point "B"). In order to complete this task, however, the disciples had to proceed with the following multi-step directions:

> Step 1- They had to go to the city.
> Step 2- They had to wait for a man carrying a jar of water to find them.
> Step 3- They had to follow him.
> Step 4- They had to enter into the house that this man entered.
> Step 5- They had to tell the master of the house, "The teacher says, 'Where is my guest room where I may eat the Passover with my Disciples?'"
> Step 6- They had to follow the man into the large upper room that would be furnished and ready.
> Step 7- They had to make the preparations there.

The results of these steps would eventually be the Last Supper.

†††

In our learning environments, we are required to ensure that our students are capable of completing multi-step directions like these. It is a valuable life skill that begins in primary school and carries on through the rest of our lives.

In our faith, we know that our journey from point "A" to point "B" both starts and ends with Jesus. Like the disciples who followed Jesus' directions, the steps we take in guiding our students toward the direction of Jesus will ultimately reflect our obedience. When we have prepared a place for Him in our learning environments, He will take them by the hand to finally finish with them at point "B": heaven.

74. The Art of Question Asking

And as he sat on the Mount of Olives opposite the tem-
ple, Peter and James and John and Andrew asked him
privately, "Tell us, when will this be, and what will be
the sign when these things are all to be accomplished?"
- Mark 13:3-4

The apostles had many doubts as a result of questions from the Master. Many of these doubts were internalized over the course of their time with Jesus. We find them reacting to these doubts outwardly by asking their Master questions that they had come up with on their own.

The types of questions that we ask can result in the type of critical thinking skills our students exercise. For that reason, it is imperative that we know, understand, and put into practice the various methods of question asking. A couple important question types are:

- Simple questions: allow students to build their study skills and memory; to recall answers that have already been studied exhaustively.
- Seek and find questions: motivational questions; to find the answer, the students must research various sources.
- Critical thinking questions: make the students think outside the box so that the student will be able to internalize the concepts we attempt to teach them.

†††

When our questions are asked at the right time and with the correct tone, they have the ability to open the minds of our youth and challenge them to think in new ways. When we teach them how to identify and ask these questions in the same way, they, like the apostles, will be able to individualize the lessons and make sense of the information in their own brains.

Guided by the Spirit, our questions will make our students think so deeply that they will not need to hear our answers. Rather, they will motivate them to come up with their own.

75. Modeling

And they were on the road, going up to Jerusalem, and Jesus was walking ahead of them; and they were amazed, and those who followed were afraid. And taking the twelve again, he began to tell them what was to happen to him, saying, "Behold, we are going up to Jerusalem; and the Son of man will be delivered to the chief priests and the scribes, and they will condemn him to death, and deliver him to the Gentiles; and they will mock him, and spit upon him, and scourge him, and kill him; and after three days he will rise."
- Mark 10:32-34

The context of St. Mark's gospel reading consists of Jesus' first step in the direction of Jerusalem. This is the place where He will be turned in by His own friend, judged unjustly, and suffer before being put to death on the cross. As He and His apostles walk around the outskirts of the city, He pulls them aside and reminds them for a third time of what will happen to Him. Still unable to comprehend what Jesus is trying to teach them, they are confused by His directions.

Many times as educators, we fall into this same dilemma. We explain orally what we want our students to do and this practice tends to result in more questions than actual progress. We find ourselves repeating our directions and answering the same question several times. We ask ourselves, "Why can't they just do what I told them to do?"

†††

Jesus was in the same dilemma before entering into Jerusalem. To make Himself clear, He had to actually show His disciples exactly what He meant. He had to go through the process of His Passion step by step so that His students could see, experience, and understand His oral directions. This process is called modeling, and we should do it every day in our learning environments if we want our students to truly understand what we are asking them to do.

If we want to make our directions clear, let's do what Jesus did: announce them orally, model them, and have them available in written form. Let's not be frustrated if we need to repeat the directions a couple of times so that our students can understand. After all, Jesus still repeats Himself every day when He calls on His children. Why should we be so different?

76. Having "Eyes in the Back of our Heads"

Many of the Jews therefore, who had come with Mary and had seen what he did, believed in him; but some of them went to the Pharisees and told them what Jesus had done. So the chief priests and the Pharisees gathered the council, and said, "What are we to do? For this man performs many signs. If we let him go on thus, every one will believe in him, and the Romans will come and destroy both our holy place * and our nation." But one of them, Caiaphas, who was high

priest that year, said to them, "You know nothing at all; you do not understand that it is expedient for you that one man should die for the people, and that the whole nation should not perish."
- John 11:45-50

The cookie jar was such a wonderful temptation when we were kids. It gleamed from above the top shelf of our cabinets and beckoned every boy and girl who crossed its path to come and eat of its deliciousness. Of course, getting to the top of this apex was the task that all of our shortness could not wait to take on. We'd open drawers and begin our summit when, from the other side of the house, would come the words from our parents that would stop us in our tracks, "(your name), did you ask permission to get a cookie?"

"How did she know?" we would ponder. "It's like she has eyes all over the place!"

Effective teachers are known for being able to foresee poor decisions being made by their students even when their students don't think they are watching. They read social situations and physical cues to a point that they can feel specific thoughts in the air. It is then they are considered to have "eyes in the back of their heads" like the parent who called out our cookie fetishes.

†††

Jesus has eyes only for souls. While He speaks about His imminent suffering, His enemies were plotting as to how they would confirm these premonitions. Jesus, with the powers of divine nature, knew this, but with the obedience of His human nature, accepted this.

As a Christian teacher in full union with His Church, you have this same ability. You benefit from the Master's spiritual graces which means that you too have eyes for souls. Indeed, with the Master's help, you can see your students for what they truly are, what God meant them to be, even if they haven't discovered it yet.

77. Using Idioms

And taking the twelve, he said to them, "Behold, we are going up to Jerusalem, and everything that is written of the Son of man by the prophets will be accomplished. For he will be delivered to the Gentiles, and will be mocked and shamefully treated and spit upon; they will scourge him and kill him, and on the third day he will rise." But they understood none of these things; this saying was hid from them, and they did not grasp what was said.
- Luke 18:31-34

Idioms blend so commonly into our conversations that we rarely stop to think about how incredibly obtuse they are. We clamor that it is raining "cats and dogs" or that if we fail at completing a task twice, we will be successful on our next attempt because "the third time's a charm." Is it really raining cats and dogs? Is it because we failed twice that we will be successful on our third attempt? No. Do we ever stop to think about these phrases after we say them? Probably not.

By definition, idioms are expressions whose meaning is not predictable from the usual meanings of its constituent elements.[58] What strikes me is why we use them in the first place. Why would anyone use an expression that has a different meaning than the one intended if they want to get their point across?

---

58 *Literarydevices.net* (4 Jan 2015) at http://literarydevices.net/idiom/

After doing a little research, it turns out that each idiom has an interesting story behind it, one that creatively intertwines meaning with cultural history.

For example, when we say it is "raining cats and dogs," we must return back to 17th century England to find its origin. The U.K. phrase finder comments:

"...in the filthy streets of 17th/18th century England, heavy rain would occasionally carry along dead animals and other debris. The animals didn't fall from the sky, but the sight of dead cats and dogs floating by in storms could well have caused the coining of this colourful phrase."[59]

"The third time is a charm" has an interesting story behind it too. Wiki.answers states: "...it alludes to the belief that, under English law, anyone who survived three attempts at hanging would be set free. This is probably from the story of John 'Babbacombe' Lee."[60]

†††

We use idioms more often than we realize. If we can linguistically mutter something so arbitrary such as an idiom in our daily language without knowing that we are using them or understanding where their meanings come from, it makes me wonder if we go through something similar with our spirituality. Do I imitate Christ without realizing it? Can I be like Him even if I don't fully understand Him?

The answer to these questions is "yes." The more we allow Jesus to work through us, the more profound His hold on us becomes. Through His power, we constantly complete His work and most times we do it without even knowing it. As a result, we dive deeper into the mystery of love which manifests itself in our giving, but we will never fully comprehend it while living.

---

59 *The Phrase Finder* (29 June 2012) at http://www.phrases.org.uk
60 *Wiki Answers* (29 June 2012) at http://wiki.answers.com

In the reading, Jesus told His disciples for the third time in the Gospel of Matthew that He would need to give it all on the cross. Indeed, "the third time was a charm."

78. Using the Method of Music

And many spread their garments on the road, and others spread leafy branches which they had cut from the fields. And those who went before and those who followed cried out, "Hosanna! Blessed is he who comes in the name of the Lord! Blessed is the kingdom of our father David that is coming! Hosanna in the highest!" And he entered Jerusalem, and went into the temple; and when he had looked round at everything, as it was already late, he went out to Bethany with the twelve.
- Mark 11:8-11

Thanks to modern media, we are exposed to more music than any other generation before us. Because of such exposure, it is not uncommon to see our youth reciting the lines to the most recent hit with perfect rhythm and striking clarity. Having heard the song many times, they have taken the liberty of memorizing every word and singing them with confidence.

This same confidence can be transferred to our students' learning by using music in our lessons. By putting some of our lessons into rhythm and rhyme, we can have our students singing their education with the same excitement and clarity as they do when they sing along to the most recent hit.

The research supports this method as well. Here is what the National Center for Biotechnology Information has to say about the influence that music plays on education: "Music automatically awakes us, arouses us and engenders specific emotions in us, which in turn modulates and controls many cognitive functions."[61]

†††

As we can see, the method of music touches our emotions and stimulates our minds. That's why there is a great population of people in the United States who would prefer to sing their ABCs as opposed to saying them. That is also why the people welcomed Jesus to Jerusalem with song, because they were emotionally stimulated to do so.

If we wish for our students to get emotionally stimulated about their education, why not utilize the teaching method of song? It has been proven scientifically and spiritually to be effective.

79. Leaving an Impression

So Jesus again said to them, "Truly, truly, I say to you, I am the door of the sheep. All who came before me are thieves and robbers; but the sheep did not heed them. I am the door; if any one enters by me, he will be saved, and will go in and out and find pasture. The thief comes only to steal and kill and destroy; I came that they may have life, and have it abundantly. I am the good shepherd. The good shepherd lays down his life for the sheep. He who is a hireling and not a shepherd, whose own the sheep are not, sees the wolf coming and leaves the sheep and flees; and the wolf snatches them and scatters them. He flees because he is a hireling and cares nothing for the sheep. I am the good shepherd;

61 Lutz Jäncke, "Music, memory and emotion". *The National Center for Biotechnology Information J Biol.* 2008; 7(6): 21 BioMed Central Ltd (8 August 2008) at http://www.ncbi.nlm.nih.gov/

I know my own and my own know me, as the Father knows me and I know the Father; and I lay down my life for the sheep. And I have other sheep, that are not of this fold; I must bring them also, and they will heed my voice. So there shall be one flock, one shepherd. For this reason the Father loves me, because I lay down my life, that I may take it again. No one takes it from me, but I lay it down of my own accord. I have power to lay it down, and I have power to take it again; this charge I have received from my Father."
- John 10:7-18

Cattle herders have a distinct manner of marking their animals. First, they heat up a steel poker that usually has some sort of design on its tip. Then, they sear a part of their animals' bodies with this poker so that if they ever were to escape or intermingle with another herd, they can be identified as property of the owner by their tattoo-like scars.

Jesus does something similar to His "herd," Christians. In fact, He literally compares us to His herd. Since He is the Good Shepherd, He has seared His flock to make sure that we can be identified as His when we intermingle with the evils of the world. This mark is our faith, and we choose to show it proudly so all can see, or hide it in fear of what others might think of us.

††††

As educators, we develop a similar "mark" within our teaching that we hope to impress upon our students. Granted, we don't stab them with a hot poker like animals, nor are we able to uncover their faith against their own will. We are, however, able to teach in ways that help them understand the world and their faith on a deeper level. If we succeed in teaching not only the worldly truths that our subjects require us to teach, but also the spiritual truths that our God requires us to teach, we will surely see our students bearing the marks of our instruction in their daily lives.

If we wish to leave this impression on them, we must listen to Jesus' advice. We must be wise as serpents and simple as doves. We must not worry about what we are to say but let the Spirit speak through us. We must endure to the end so that all may be saved. If we do all of this according to God's will, we will become like our Shepherd, our students will become like us, and all will bear His mark upon our souls.

However, like a cattle herder's hot poker, this will hurt.

80. Defining Freedom, Facts and Opinions

At that time Herod the tetrarch heard about the fame of Jesus; and he said to his servants, "This is John the Baptist, he has been raised from the dead; that is why these powers are at work in him."
- Matt. 14:1-2

King Herod is stuck in the middle of that labyrinth. Instead of researching the facts, he defers to his royal opinion of who he *thinks* Jesus is. This knowledge based on a mere supposition led to his worry and grief, for he surely thought that a resurrected John the Baptist would take vengeance on him for ending his life unjustly. Little did he know that the key to life was the very Man he mistook for John the Baptist: Jesus.

What an immense error on the king's part! Jesus was the Son of God and could easily have calmed the king's worry with just one stretch of his forgiving hands. Indeed the poor king's conscience was troubled by our Lord when he easily could have been freed from the chains of guilt if he would have only pursued the facts.

†††

Today's students are exposed to more information than any generation before. They can access the Internet and have answers to any of their questions in seconds. However, they are also bombarded with a plethora of opinions from strangers who can now create their own blog, website etc. and post whatever interpretation of truth they think is correct. Much like king Herod, the truth is hidden from them under the cloud of various opinions, including their own.

It is our job to educate our students on how to tell the difference between what is fact and what is opinion. To do this, we must expose them to both facts and opinions on a regular basis. Then, we must lead them to discover the authentic source of the information being shared. Finally, we must guide them as to how they can place themselves in the author's shoes based on the circumstances in which they published their information.

81. Joining the Winning Team

Now when Jesus came into the district of Caesarea Philippi, he asked his disciples, "Who do men say that the Son of man is?" And they said, "Some say John the Baptist, others say Elijah, and others Jeremiah or one of the prophets." He said to them, "But who do you say that I am?" Simon Peter replied, "You are the Christ, the Son of the living God." And Jesus answered him, "Blessed are you, Simon Bar-Jona! For flesh and blood has not revealed this to you, but my Father who is in heaven. And I tell you, you are Peter, and on this rock I will build my church, and the powers of death shall not prevail against it. I will give you the keys of the king-

*dom of heaven, and whatever you bind on earth shall
be bound in heaven, and whatever you loose on earth
shall be loosed in heaven." Then he strictly charged
the disciples to tell no one that he was the Christ.*
- Matt. 16:13-20

Jesus founded one Church. This is a Biblical fact that many
people overlook. He established Peter as the leadership of His
Church and promised two things:

1. "The gates of death shall not prevail against it."
2. To the apostles, specifically Peter, He said that "whatever you bind on earth shall be bound in heaven; and
whatever you loose on earth shall be loosed in heaven,"
thus giving them authority over His Church.

If you are a Christian, you are an integral part of this living,
breathing Church. Some call it an institution, others call it a set of
rules and doctrines, but Catholic teachers know that true Christianity, like education, merely begins with these common procedures. The real meat of it all is deeply rooted in a relationship.

Christ asks us to ponder who exactly He is. He also com-
forts us by leaving an authority on earth to guide us towards the
immovable Rock of Truth. The more we learn about this Church
and the authorities that guide it, the closer we come to knowing its
head, Christ. His is the relationship that guides us, the Captain that
chose us to be a part of the winning team.

†††

Our students ask themselves this same question about us every time they step into our learning environments. Who is this
person? Why is he/she here? Why should I bother listening to

him/her?

If we teach correctly, they will know which team we play for. As a result of our contagious love, they will want with a deep passion to be a part of that team because they will know that by being a part of it, they will not lose.

But before we can establish this student-teacher relationship, we must first become a part of something much bigger than ourselves, the one, holy, catholic and apostolic Church that was formed by Christ's relationship with Peter and the rest of His apostles over 2,000 years ago. Crossing the Tiber is the first step towards attaining perfect grace through Christ's beloved Bride, His Church.

82. Tipping Point

And as some spoke of the temple, how it was adorned with noble stones and offerings, he said, "As for these things which you see, the days will come when there shall not be left here one stone upon another that will not be thrown down."
- Luke 21:5-6

Jesus ransacked the money changers from the temple,[62] cursed the fig tree,[63] and yelled at His disciples for their unbelief.[64] This day, He let loose on the Pharisees' business-hold over Jerusalem.

Sometimes our students simply deserve a good tongue lashing. The frustration of poor behavior and lazy performances on tasks is simply unacceptable. It is when our reachable expecta-

---

62 Matt. 21:12
63 Matt. 21:18-22
64 Matt. 17:17

tions are not met due to no fault of our own that we, like Jesus, lose it.

†††

At times, it is good to let your students know you are upset. But if we want to do it right, we need to be sure that we have taken every possible opportunity to deliver our message clearly. If the message is still not captured, then we are at spiritual liberty to explode provided our consciences are clean and the time is right.

One last note: Don't let your tipping point take away from your joy. May your chides be as few and far between as Jesus' reprimands and perhaps then your miracles will be as numerous as His.

83. Waking Up

And there will be signs in sun and moon and stars, and upon the earth distress of nations in perplexity at the roaring of the sea and the waves, men fainting with fear and with foreboding of what is coming on the world; for the powers of the heavens will be shaken. And then they will see the Son of man coming in a cloud with power and great glory. Now when these things begin to take place, look up and raise your heads, because your redemption is drawing near.
- Luke 21:25-28

Every fall we thank God that the earth's axis is tilted and that my country participates in the practice of daylight savings time. We can revel in His gifts of recreation, leisure and sleep for 60 more minutes because of this glorious concept.

On the flip side, springing ahead as the flowers begin to bloom after spring's daylight savings change is like the thief who came in the night and stole your sleep when you most desperately needed it; at the end of the school year!

For weeks after daylight savings time switches, we can feel the effects of what gaining/losing an hour does to our bodies and minds. We see how nature becomes darker/lighter when we wake up and view different skies than we are accustomed to.

†††

Jesus describes a time of similar exhaustive disconnect in this reading. However, far beyond the changes in the sun and moon, He goes further by explaining the vicious environment that will occur within nature. As He makes His warning, He calms His audience by telling them not to fear, but to raise our heads for our redemption is near.

Indeed, skies, students and our very souls experience a great shift in perception during daylight savings time. However, as awesome and horrible as they are, they are reminders of just how ready we must be for the second coming of Christ.

When you are feeling exhausted from your daily toil and your bed tempts you to remain snuggled up in its comfort and warmth, wake up. Your work, and consequently your redemption and the redemption of all of your students, is at hand.

84. Choosing One Thing, Not One More Thing

*And he told them a parable: "Look at the fig tree, and
all the trees; as soon as they come out in leaf, you see
for yourselves and know that the summer is already
near. So also, when you see these things taking place,*

you know that the kingdom of God is near. Truly, I say
to you, this generation will not pass away till all has
taken place. Heaven and earth will pass away, but my
words will not pass away."
- Luke 21:29-33

Take a moment and attempt to remember each and every one of your past teachers. Now, it is probable that while you were thinking, a few of your favorite teachers popped into your head and, perhaps a few of the bad ones. Go deeper now. What exactly do you remember about those good/bad teachers?

Odds are, your memory became a pool of generalized memories about that person. Right in the middle of this pool there was one thing that made them stand out amongst the generalities, one thing that made their existence important in your life.

It may have been the time you were ridiculed in front of your peers, the time you were congratulated for your achievements or the many hours of one-on-one time that this person sacrificed because they saw something special in you.

†††

In the same way that "heaven and earth will pass away, but [Jesus'] words will not pass away," so too will the memory of every lesson you taught your students pass away. What will remain is this one thing.

85. Letting Go

"Let not your hearts be troubled; believe in God, be-
lieve also in me. In my Father's house are many rooms;
if it were not so, would I have told you that I go to

prepare a place for you? And when I go and prepare a place for you, I will come again and will take you to myself, that where I am you may be also. And you know the way where I am going." Thomas said to him, "Lord, we do not know where you are going; how can we know the way?" Jesus said to him, "I am the way, and the truth, and the life; no one comes to the Father, but by me. If you had known me, you would have known my Father also; henceforth you know him and have seen him.
- John 14:1-7

There comes a time for every teacher when we give an assignment to our students that we know they will be unable to complete because we haven't really taught them how to do it yet. This can occur for many reasons: absent students, underperformance, forgetfulness and perhaps to gage our students' ability to work independently are just a few. In any of these cases, we ask our students to "go it alone" and we are fairly confident that they will be unsuccessful.

Up until this point in the reading, Jesus has been close to His apostles throughout the entire Gospel. Sure, He left them in the raging waters, but He returned to calm the sea. He left to pray alone, but He always came back to guide them in faith.

†††

At this point in the Gospel, He begins to let loose of this spiritual grasp so that His followers, especially Peter, will learn to go it alone. He was sure that their faith would be shaken, that they would fail at first, but He was confident that after the initial shock of His death, the lessons that He taught them would come full circle when He returned to them on the day of His resurrection

140

and, more profoundly on the day of Pentecost.

Students need to learn to work independently. We must give them this opportunity when we know they are ready to receive it. Granted, their worlds will be shaken, but their minds will surely come back to our learning environments more engaged and, like Christ, fully alive.

Let go.

86. Foreshadowing

Peter said to him, "Even though they all fall away, I will not." And Jesus said to him, "Truly, I say to you, this very night, before the cock crows twice, you will deny me three times." But he said vehemently, "If I must die with you, I will not deny you." And they all said the same.
- Mark 14:29-31

One of the reading skills we try to impress upon our students is that of foreshadowing. Foreshadowing is when we make predictions to help us better understand the text. In making predictions, we become more involved in the text and anticipate its results with imagination, logic, and reasoning.

Apart from reading, we use foreshadowing in our daily lives as well. Take for example, our weekly meals. Before we go grocery shopping, we think ahead about what meals we want to cook throughout the week. These predictions help us organize our grocery list and allot a certain amount of our paycheck to the purchase of these products.

†††

Jesus foreshadows Peter's denial. Although Peter is stubborn in his response to such a frightful prediction, Jesus remains firm. The result is Peter's realization of his errors and his complete understanding of Jesus as Lord. Although he had to go through the path of sin and denial, when all was said and done he was able to return to his Master.

We are like Jesus in that we have the ability to see what paths our students are heading down. Some are on the road to success where others are, like Peter, heading towards a path of destruction. In the same way Jesus saved Peter by foretelling his denial, so too are we able to alert our students of the effects of the avenues they are taking. As much as we strive to steer our students towards the correct path, it is ultimately they who are in the drivers' seats.

87. Just Between You and Me

He rose from supper, laid aside his garments, and gird-
ed himself with a towel. Then he poured water into a
basin, and began to wash the disciples' feet, and to
wipe them with the towel with which he was girded.
- John 13:4-5

There once was a man who chose to have "the talk" with his son. Since his son was maturing into a young man, he felt it was the right time. The only problem was that he didn't know just how to get the message across. He had never had "the talk" with his father, so he himself really didn't know what to say.

After praying about it, he had an idea. He would take his son, a lover of sport, to a professional basketball game that would require a three hour drive. For three hours, He would open up conversation and talk about "the birds and the bees" with his son then capitalize on their common interest by screaming their heads off in a packed area.

†††

I was the young man in the aforementioned story and I'll remember that trip as long as I live. Nothing makes life more interesting than secrets. Just-between-you-and-me conversations tend to be the ones we remember the most, even if they are embarrassing. Regardless of how we remember them, the fact that we do remember them is based on our intense desire to be loved in a personal way by somebody other than ourselves. Jesus expressed this personal love by leaning over to each of His apostles and one-by-one washing their feet.

Sitting in your learning environment are several young and eager hearts who desire with every part of their being to be loved in a personal and very unique way by their teacher. Find an opportunity today to pass them a note of congratulations, whisper a word of encouragement or invite them into the hall for a well-deserved handshake for a job well done. It will come back to you in troughs of hard work and obedience.

88. Promises

And he said to them, "This is my blood of the covenant, which is poured out for many."
- Mark 14:24

Teachers make promises. Sometimes these promises are large, like when we pledge to educate our students to the best of our abilities. Other promises are small like when we tell our students things like "Only five more minutes to finish up what you are working on," or "If your behavior is good this week we might be able to have our class outside." Regardless of their size, the promises we make become sacred to our students and fulfilling them is primary.

A lot of times we make these promises with little realization. For example, when a student asks us a question and we don't know the answer, we may say something like, "I do not know the answer to that question, but I will look it up and see what I can find." Our next step will show whether or not we are teachers of our word. We can either forget about it or make a quick note to remind us to find the information.

†††

Jesus makes a covenant, which is a synonym for "contract," in the shedding of His blood. Meant to be a gift for His people, this cup of wine was depicting the blood that would actually flow in His eventual death. In His Passion, Jesus fulfilled this promise of the shedding of His blood and completed His words with the most selfless act the world has ever known.

As we reflect on the promises we make in our learning environments, let us first think about whether or not we have the ability to fulfill them. The book of James advises us to "Let [our] 'yes' be 'yes' and [our]'no' be 'no.'"[65] When we do decide to make promises, both small and large, may we complete them in the same way Jesus did – by putting our words into actions. Only then will our students be able to understand the difference between an empty promise and a full one.

89. Unorthodox Orthodoxy

And he took bread, and when he had given thanks he broke it and gave it to them, saying, "This is my body which is given for you. Do this in remembrance of me."

---

65 James 5:12

And likewise the cup after supper, saying, "This cup which is poured out for you is the new covenant in my blood."
- Luke 22:19-20

During the past few centuries, humanity has shifted our philosophical beliefs towards relativism. Relativism deems personal interpretations of truth as acceptable. In essence, we become our own islands of thought, each with their own custom-made creed and judgment.

We say things like "All religions lead to heaven," and "You can believe whatever you want" when, in the depths of our being we know these comments to be false. If such claims were true, then the actions of the Klu Klux Klan would be permissible and your very own spouse could secretly commit adultery and would never need to seek your forgiveness to be considered free from moral error. If we all base "truth" on our personal opinions, cohesion cannot exist. There simply must be an anchor for morality!

Our moment in time is not so different from Jesus'. Jewish Law became relativistic and contrite in much the same way as our pop-culture society. His response: unexpected orthodoxy.

†††

Jesus' sacrifice at the table and on the cross is the catalyst that leads to the apex of His mission: the resurrection. His act of establishing the New Passover shows just how loyal he was to truth and how ludicrous the world thought of such spiritual practices. When we act in communion with Him during the Liturgy of the Eucharist, we rip ourselves away from the relativist beliefs of society and unite our souls with the immovable Truth in the Person of Christ who declared:

"Unless you eat the flesh of the Son of Man and drink his

blood, you do not have life within you. Whoever eats my flesh and drinks my blood has eternal life, and I will raise him on the last day. For my flesh is true food, and my blood is true drink. Whoever eats my flesh and drinks my blood remains in me and I in him. "[66]

As you teach today, society will tell your students to believe in something trivial and meaningless. Through your action and instruction, you have the power to remove them from their relativism because you are connected through the Eucharist to the Anchor of Truth: Jesus Christ.

90. Judases

Then one of the twelve, who was called Judas Iscariot, went to the chief priests and said, "What will you give me if I deliver him to you?" And they paid him thirty pieces of silver. And from that moment he sought an opportunity to betray him.
- Matt. 26:14-16

In some ways, we are no better than Judas. We stumble and eventually mess everything up. We sin and we do it more than we even realize.

It is important to remember that Jesus chose Judas to be one of His closest followers. Being all-knowing and all-powerful, Jesus could not have chosen Judas as a slight error in His salvific plan. Judas and his betrayal were part of God's plan for our salvation.

To this day, the weeds of betrayal continue to grow among the roots of His perfect foliage. Judases are always among us painting a counterfeit copy of truth that goes directly against the message we are teaching our students. As a result, we put up with the insults, the pain and the embarrassment of being servants to

---

66 John 6:53-56

humanity. Perhaps that's how our Lord felt as He hung from the cross?

†††

That's where you come in. You have also been called by Christ to complete His mission of educating souls. Like Judas, you fail because of sin, but like Jesus, you are able to encourage "so that we may be able to encourage those who are in any affliction with the encouragement with which we ourselves are encouraged by God."[67]

We will continue to suffer at the hands of the Judases of the world. However, we don't have to accept the sinful lifestyle as the norm. On the contrary, it is our duty to fight against the tide of sin in order to reach paradise with all of those who are willing to follow us.

What better place to start than in your classroom?

91. The Gift of Suffering

Then Pilate took Jesus and had him flogged... So they took Jesus, and he went out, bearing his own cross, to the place called the place of a skull, which is called in Hebrew Golgotha. There they crucified him, and with him two others, one on either side, and Jesus between them.
- John 19:1, 17-18

Many times, we see suffering as a negative aspect of life. We tend to believe that suffering is a punishment or a problem that needs to be fixed in our lives. When we look at suffering through

---

67 2 Cor. 1:4

our own eyes, the only aspect we can recognize may be what is negative about it. Whatever hurts our senses or feelings tends to ignite what is selfish and defiant within us.

But suffering is something much more than that. When we look at suffering through the eyes of Christ crucified, we can see it as a sacrifice of self, a heroic action for the enlightenment of truth, a light that brightens our souls in service.

†††

Mother Teresa of Calcutta once made the following statement about the "gift" of suffering.

"I wonder what the world would be like if there were not innocent people making reparation for us all? Today the Passion of Christ is being relived in the lives of those who suffer. To accept that suffering is a gift of God. Suffering is not a punishment. Jesus does not punish. Suffering is a sign – a sign that we have come so close to Jesus on the cross that he can kiss us, show us that he is in love with us by giving us an opportunity to share in his Passion. Suffering is not a punishment, nor a fruit of sin; it is a gift of God. He allows us to share in his suffering and to make up for the sins of the world."[68]

Mother Teresa was given this gift as a Missionary of Charity. Jesus was given this gift upon the cross. How much more thankful should we be to experience such a gift from God as suffering? How much more of a gift is it to help our students understand its spiritual value?

This is the secret to Christian happiness: that even in our darkness we can find the light of joy.

---

68 Mother Theresa, & S. P. Lovett, editor, *Best Gift of Love* (Ann Arbor, MI: Servant Publications, 1993)

92. Why?

And about the ninth hour Jesus cried with a loud voice,
"Eli, Eli, lama sabach-thani?" that is, "My God, my
God, why hast thou forsaken me?"
- Matt. 27:46

When children reach a certain age, they fall in love with the question "Why?" They ask questions like "Why is the sky blue?" and "Why do I have to go to sleep?" They use it at every moment in faith of knowing that the adults they ask will have the right answer. Although this might be bothersome to us at times, it is one of the greatest teaching strategies ever created.

Jesus asks this question from the cross, "Why?" In His eternal wisdom, surely He knew what His fate would be and that not even His own plea for help would be answered. However, He still called out to His Father and asked why He had to suffer, why He had to die, why His Father would let this happen?

††††

Like Jesus, our students are full of "Why's" that they don't fully comprehend. The older they get, the more complex they become. They yearn to return to those days when they could ask their family and friends "Why?" and receive a believable answer.

We are the best resource that our students have in helping them contemplate their reasons for living. To unlock these profound thoughts, all we need to do is revert back to our childhood curiosity and ask the question, "Why?" Doing so will allow our supplication to be joined with Jesus' as He hung on the cross.

93. Personal Deaths

*When Jesus had received the vinegar, he said, "It is fin-
ished"; and he bowed his head and gave up his spirit.*
- John 19:30

Death has a way of changing the world. When a living being leaves us the world becomes a different place in two ways:
because of its absence, and because of its memory. My childhood
dog is no longer physically here to jump into my arms or bark at
every visitor that walks through the door. However, she remains
tattooed to my memory as a treasured thought. Through her memory, her essence emits the joy of companionship and playfulness
that I will carry with me as long as I live.

†††

My dog's existence simply did not end when she died. Jesus'
didn't either. You accept personal deaths like this every day. Every
time you struggle, become disheartened and stressed, you take up
your cross and carry it through Calvary. Like Christ, you are able
to take the difficulties of your day and "complete what is lacking
in Christ's afflictions for the sake of his body."[69]
When the day is over, we too are able to say with Christ, "It
is finished." However, we know that the essence of our hard work
and dedication certainly does not stop there. Like Jesus, our love
endures forever in the hearts of those we have taught.

94. "Ah Ha!" Moments

And when the centurion, who stood facing him, saw

---

69 Col. 1:24

*that he thus breathed his last, he said, "Truly this man
was the Son of God!"*
- Mark 15:39

Our students take time to process information. Some take
more time than others. For that reason, it is always a great joy to
watch what happens shortly after a new lesson is introduced to the
class. Like light bulbs turning on above their heads, some students
mechanically utter "Ohhhhhhh," when they finally grasp the idea
and are excited to be able to put it into practice. We call these moments of pure teaching pleasure, "Ah ha" moments.

These are the moments we live for as educators. We plan,
explain, engage, explore, tutor, lecture, and complete every other
action under the sun so that these moments can happen. What's
more is that we pray in hopes that "Ah ha" moments happen not
only for our students, but for us as well.

†††

The Roman Centurion had his own "Ah ha" moment. No
more than hours ago, soldiers like this man were mocking the dy-
ing Jesus along with the rest of the crowd. As this particular Centurion stood facing the lifeless body of Christ, he became the first
fruit of salvation and became the first Roman believer. This "Ah
ha" moment was invaluable to the Centurion's soul.

Jesus tells us, "[we] are the light of the world."[70] I like to
believe that the source of this light comes from the light bulbs that
turn on above our heads during the "Ah ha" moments of our lives.
The more moments, the more light is given off. Before this light
can be bright, Jesus Himself must turn it on. Take a moment to be
in silence with Him today so that He can flip the switch on for us
and for our students.

---

70 Matt. 5:14

OUR CONTINUING EDUCATION

A teacher's job never ends. Even after we retire, we continue to learn and teach our newfound knowledge to anyone who's willing to consult our wisdom. We might not see the fruits of our labor soon, or ever, but through faith we know that our toil was meaningful.

If you don't know this now, it will make complete sense when we enter those pearly gates and see Him. My hope is that He says to you, "Well done, good and faithful servant."[71]

These final Gospel reflections speak of Christ's own continuing education that took place after His resurrection. They serve as a starting point for your own journey towards the glorious entry into His celestial home both "on earth as it is in heaven."[72]

95. Teaching Without Ceasing

And Jesus said to them, "A prophet is not without honor, except in his own country, and among his own kin, and in his own house." And he could do no mighty

71 Matt. 25:21
72 Matt. 6:10

work there, except that he laid his hands upon a few
sick people and healed them. And he marveled because
of their unbelief. And he went about among the villages
teaching.
- Mark 16:4-6

Christ was laid inside a tomb for three days. No biblical record indicates that He completed any *earthly* work during
this time. However, according to the Catechism of the Catholic
Church, "...the crucified one sojourned in the realm of the dead
prior to his resurrection... Jesus, like all men, experienced death
and in his soul joined the others in the realm of the dead. But
he descended there as Savior, proclaiming the Good News to the
spirits imprisoned there."[73]

During Christ's three days of death, His soul continued to
work. Even when He was seemingly *absent* to those who knew
Him, He was fully *present* to those He was saving in Sheol. As a
result of this saving of the *dead*, He began His preparations for the
salvation of the *living*.

†††

Teachers can relate with this type of disconnect quite easily.
When our students are working, or even when we are instructing
them, we subconsciously store their current progress within our
minds. When the school day is over and instruction has stopped,
we constantly descend into our own subconscious and find our
students' current levels of understanding there. Like Christ, we
then begin preparations for their future lessons that will ultimately
resurrect their levels of understanding the next time we come back
to their presence.

---

73 *Catechism of the Catholic Church,* 2nd ed. (Washington, DC: United States
Catholic Conference, 2000), 632

The job of a teacher is never finished. Our school day never ends with our final lesson. Like Christ, our minds, bodies and souls are dedicated to the advancement of souls and for that reason, even when we are absent from our students, our souls are fully present making preparations for their education.

96. Coming Full Circle

Now the eleven disciples went to Galilee, to the mountain to which Jesus had directed them. And when they saw him they worshipped him; but some doubted. And Jesus came and said to them, "All authority in heaven and on earth has been given to me. Go therefore and make disciples of all nations, baptizing them in the name of the Father and of the Son and of the Holy Spirit, teaching them to observe all that I have commanded you; and lo, I am with you always, to the close of the age."
- Matt. 28:16-20

There are no words that can describe the sensation a teacher feels when, after countless hours of planning and a careful delivery, one of our lessons comes full circle and makes an unforgettable impact on our students' minds. Once we have achieved this feeling of teaching euphoria, it becomes so addictive that we attempt this same outcome with all of our lessons.

It is fitting that Jesus comes full circle with His mission of proclaiming the Gospel message to His disciples and to the world. We might recall that on the first day of His mission, we met Jesus' disciples, they were fearful, over passionate, and at times, ignorant. Since meeting Jesus, they were transformed into the fearless, patient, and wise men and women we see proclaiming the Gospel message in all places. Jesus watched them take His lessons and apply them directly to their lives, even when they are doubtful. In fact, He worked with them to make sure this would happen and confirmed the word through accompanying signs.

†††

We have come to the realization that we also work with Jesus every day in our learning environments. Through this book, we have learned to share in the same educational vocation of the Master. Each reflection has described the methodological, pedagogical, and spiritual parallels that our instructional work shares with the ministry of Jesus. By putting them into practice, we allow ourselves to come full circle with Jesus in regard to our relationship with Him and His mission for us.

Part of accomplishing that mission with your students is creating a moment in each class that you are able to come full circle with them. The best way to do this is to look back at the progress they have made since the beginning of the academic year. Examples of how to do this include creating lists of concepts learned, reviewing goals that had been set in the past and contemplating ones to achieve in the future.

As we learned in the previous lesson, our work with our students is never complete. Granted, our students will eventually leave us and use the lessons we've taught them to achieve success in the world. However, our work will eventually come full circle when we meet again in heaven.

97. You Can't Do It All

But there are also many other things which Jesus did; were every one of them to be written, I suppose that the

world itself could not contain the books that would be written.
- John 21:25

What Jesus said and did during His three year ministry were countless. That is what St. John is tells us as his final sentence. An entire world filled with books about Jesus' life could not fit his eternal impact on the world. So, why should our teaching be any different?

Teachers like to think that the entire world depends on them. We stay up late correcting papers and writing lesson plans not because we don't have anything better to do, but because we believe that we can make a difference.

†††

We believe Mother Teresa when she says "We ourselves feel that what we are doing is just a drop in the ocean. But the ocean would be less because of that missing drop."[74] We find ourselves pulling out the garden hose, waiting underneath the rain gutters with a bucket and filling up our super soakers every moment we get so as to empty into the endless abyss of Christ's love.

Even then, we never think it is enough. We still collapse with emotion every time we make a mistake or, worse yet, watch our students make them. Jesus' response is simple. Of the infinite amount of good that He did during His ministry, not even He, the Son of God, could convert the world.

98. What We Can Do, We Do It Amazingly

Truly, truly, I say to you, he who believes in me will

---

74 Sy Safransky, *Sunbeams, Revised Edition: A Book of Quotations* (Berkley, CA: North Atlantic Books, 2012)

also do the works that I do; and greater works than
these will he do, because I go to the Father.
- John 14:12

The word of God has a lasting effect on the world. He said "let there be light,"[75] and there was light. Holding the bread and wine He said "This is my body" and "this is my blood,"[76] and we receive Him in the Eucharist every time we celebrate the Mass.

When He says, then, that we will do greater works than those that He did, what does that mean? It means that You already benefit from a multitude of graces because you share in His same profession of Teacher. You have been given specific gifts to use and motivation to develop your talents. You have been blessed to guide the most valuable asset of His Church, the youth. You have an infinite amount of ways to communicate His message of love.

†††

The words of God are constantly working through you. In the words of Isaiah, "Yet just as from the heavens the rain and snow come down, And do not return there till they have watered the earth, making it fertile and fruitful, Giving seed to the one who sows and bread to the one who eats, So shall my word be that goes forth from my mouth; It shall not return to me empty, but shall do what pleases me, achieving the end for which I sent it."

The expectation from Jesus is that your words and deeds be more numerous than Christ's. What He was able to accomplish in three years, you are expected to supersede during your lifetime.

Now go and do it.

---

75 Gen. 1:3

76 Luke 22:19-20

99. A Truly Catholic Education

Christ's Church is constantly instructed through Sacred Scripture. However, it also has the immense grace of sacred tradition. Through the teaching authority granted to the Apostles by Christ Himself, modern-day Bishops have been granted the graces necessary to continue the story of salvation through dogmatic declarations concerning the proper education of the Catholic faithful. One such document, *Gravissimum Educationis*, was proclaimed by Pope Paul VI in 1965. This declaration lays out a blueprint for what a truly Catholic education should look like and how we can go about making it a reality.

The first pillar of this system is parenthood. If we are concerned about the well-being and salvation of our youth, we must first ensure that our parents are properly instructed in and passionate about their Catholic faith. *Gravissimum Educationis* states that, "Parents have given children their life, they are bound by the most serious obligation to educate their offspring and therefore must be recognized as the primary and principal educators."[77]

Homeschooling parents have an immense grace in that they are not distracted by the demands of work, but are able to focus specifically on the education of their children on an individual basis. Such a Catholic education is highly beneficial for those who are able to do it. However, not all are called to this vocation.

The second pillar is civil society. "...[when] endeavors of parents and other societies are lacking, [it is the toll of civil society] to carry out the work of education in accordance with the wishes of the parents; and, moreover, as the common good demands, to build schools and institutions."[78]

The schools and institutions mentioned in the aforementioned quote refer to the invaluable vocation of public and private

---

77 *Gravissimum Educationis*, §3

78 *Gravissimum Educationis*, §Conclusion

school educators. The declaration goes on to say later that "because of a shortage of teachers, the education of youth is in jeopardy."[79] While teacher shortages are a reality due to low wages and unrealistic expectations, the more dangerous reality is that of all Catholics, educators included, roughly 7% of parishioners are doing everything in their faith community and paying almost entirely for the maintenance and mission of the Church.[80] As a result of not having the majority of well-formed adults in the Catholic faith, how could we possibly be able to form our youth?

The third and final pillar, is the Catholic Church. "...in a special way, the duty of educating belongs to the Church, not merely because she must be recognized as a human society capable of educating, but especially because she has the responsibility of announcing the way of salvation to all men, of communicating the life of Christ to those who believe, and, in her unfailing solicitude, of assisting men to be able to come to the fullness of this life."[81]

†††

The Church is the primary source of the spiritual, emotional, psychological and academic formation of her children. In her, the members of her body are attached to the saving head of Christ. Parents and teachers, especially the clergy, play *the* most pivotal role in the salvation of humanity. This is why it is imperative that we learn how to teach from the Master Teacher – Jesus.

"Beautiful indeed and of great importance is the vocation of all those who aid parents in fulfilling their duties and who, as representatives of the human community, undertake the task of education in schools. This vocation demands special qualities of

---

79 Matthew Kelly, *The Four Signs of a Dynamic Catholic* (Boston: Beaco Press, 2012)

80 *Gravissimum Educationis*, §3

81 *Gravissimum Educationis*, §Conclusion

mind and heart, very careful preparation, and continuing readiness to renew and to adapt."

Made in United States
Orlando, FL
19 January 2024

42686580R00104